Shirley Pain  She was ed at MacRob

where she was dux in 1936. She won a Senior Government Scholarship to university and was lent money by Misses Hutton, Gainfort and Lazarus of the high school to enable her to survive through her course. She graduated in Arts with Honours in 1939.

Before her marriage, she taught in state secondary schools and later in independent schools when her children were old enough to go to school.

Shirley now belongs to a film group and a reading group and is a member of a bridge club and a Probus club. She is divorced and lives in an Art Deco apartment in richly cosmopolitan St Kilda.

The Bean Patch

a memoir

SHIRLEY PAINTER

HARPER PERENNIAL

Two chapters from this book have appeared in other publications: 'The Bean
Patch' in *Quadrant*, April 1994 and 'Harry Goes West' in *Tirra Lirra*, Spring 1993.

Harper Perennial

An imprint of HarperCollins*Publishers*, Australia

First published in Australia in 2002
Reprinted in 2002 (twice)
by HarperCollins*Publishers* Pty Limited
ABN 36 009 913 517
A member of the HarperCollins*Publishers* (Australia) Pty Limited Group
www.harpercollins.com.au

HarperCollins*Publishers*
25 Ryde Road, Pymble, Sydney, NSW 2073, Australia
31 View Road, Glenfield, Auckland 10, New Zealand
77–85 Fulham Palace Road, London, W6 8JB, United Kingdom
2 Bloor Street East, 20th floor, Toronto, Ontario M4W 1A8, Canada
10 East 53rd Street, New York NY 10022, USA

National Library of Australia Cataloguing-in-Publication data:

Painter, Shirley.
    The bean patch.
    ISBN 0 7322 7421 4.
    1. Painter, Shirley - Childhood and youth. 2. Adult child
    abuse victims - Australia - Biography. 3. Abused children -
    Australia - Biography. I. Title.
    I. Title.
364.15554

Cover design by Darian Causby, HarperCollins Design Studio
Cover photograph: courtesy of the author
Author photograph: Lindsay Kelley
Typeset by HarperCollins Design Studio in 11/15 Sabon
Printed and bound in Australia by Griffin Press on 70gsm Bulky Book Ivory

7 6 5 4   06 07 08 09

Can you keep a secret?
I don't suppose you can.
You mustn't laugh,
You mustn't cry,
But do the best you can.

(OLD CHILDHOOD RHYME)

AUTHOR'S NOTE

I have changed the names of all the characters in this book out of consideration for some relatives who may not wish their names to be associated in any way with the events described in it.

Because memories are often disjointed, I had two choices in dealing with them.

The first was to tidy them all up into a neat chronological order, with a beginning, a middle and an end. But a lifetime of reading wonderful books has made me a highly critical reader, and I feared that choice might make for a very flat narrative.

The other choice was to present the reader with the same gaps, the same clues, and the same dilemmas as I had, so that the effect would be the same: What's going on? Who in this dangerous and contradictory world can be trusted? Who are the goodies in white hats and who are the baddies in black hats?

Tough, reader! I have chosen for you the hard option.

ACKNOWLEDGMENTS

My thanks are due to many friends who have borne with me when I was prickly or withdrawn or in other ways difficult as this book was being written.

To Alex Miller and Jennifer Dabbs of Holmesglen College of TAFE for their help and support.

To Dr Mollie Travers of La Trobe University, the first to assure me that my book would be published.

To my agent, Lyn Tranter, and my editors at HarperCollins, Linda Funnell, Bruce Sims and Nicola O'Shea, who have all been wonderfully constructive, compassionate and professional in their assistance.

Above all, I thank my daughters, without whose help and interaction I may never have made it.

CONTENTS

PART TWO

EPILOGUE

PROLOGUE

THE BEAN PATCH

'How WOULD you like to go for a ride with me?' asked the man in his friendly confidential way.

The little girl — she was three, going on four, big-eyed, long-haired, skinny — regarded him solemnly. She nodded, biting her thumb.

'Get her dressed!' he said to his wife. 'I want to get this over with before the shops open.'

The woman washed the sleep out of her daughter's eyes, put on the one good dress she owned, and the long white socks and the patent leather shoes that went with it.

'Stand still,' she said, 'while I brush your hair.'

Having her hair brushed was always a nightmare experience, as her mother raged through the knots and tangles. For some reason the hair always enraged her — for some deeper reason than the length or thickness or the knots. In a black-haired family she was red-haired; in a straight-haired family, hers curled.

'Beautiful!' said Grandmother.

But her mother didn't think it was beautiful.

'That hair!' she would say, as she bashed and tortured it into some sort of respectable shape. Mother was strong on respectability, and red hair, the child knew, was not respectable.

'With that hair,' said her father, 'anyone can see that she doesn't belong. She's the wrong colour.'

The child wondered where they were going, so early. On Saturday mornings they never went anywhere. Usually no-one got up till nearly lunchtime.

'Perhaps to Auntie's,' she thought hopefully. Auntie had a new black kitten and lived in a lolly shop. But she said nothing, had said nothing for a long time now.

Sometimes she woke up in the middle of the night screaming, after nightmares, and there was talk mixed up with the screaming, but nothing intelligible.

'Gibberish,' her father called it. He had a way with words, everyone said. In the daytime she said nothing to anyone.

'Funny kid,' said her father to friends and relations when they commented on her silence. 'Used to talk like a phonograph. You couldn't shut her up. Then she suddenly stopped, for no reason at all, like a tap being turned off, and we can't get a word out of her. But she's a good kid and makes no trouble. They say she'll grow out of it.'

When she was dressed, he lifted her onto the handlebars of his bicycle, and whistling cheerfully, he pedalled strongly the five miles to Richmond. The traffic was very heavy. In Bridge Road alone they passed two trams and six motor cars, and he amused himself pointing out the different makes to the child.

'That's a T-model Ford,' he said. 'That big flash one's a Chevrolet — American car. Cost a mint of money. That one's a Whippet. See that truck? I drove one like that when I was in the army. First one I've seen out here, though. Look at that motorbike! It goes without you having to pedal. I'm going to have one like that when I get my hands on some money.'

Far more interesting to the child than the cars was a milkman, late on his rounds, with his horse and cart, the horse actually dropping a great pile of steaming golden balls on the cobblestones outside the dairy.

When they got to the busy part of Richmond, the shops were already open. He stopped and lifted her down from the handlebars and led her towards the cake and tea shop on the corner.

He talked to her very quietly and seriously.

'I have to go away and buy something,' he said. 'You're to stay here till I come back. Don't move from this spot. Understand? *And don't talk to anyone.*'

She nodded. She was a good listener, from her stand of silence.

She stood outside the cake shop for a long time, without moving, almost without presence. People passed in and out of the cake shop without remarking her. She began to get hungry, and though the day was warm, she shivered. Something in her appearance attracted the attention of a woman coming out of the shop. She nudged her husband.

'See that little kid? She was standing there by herself when we come in,' she said. 'That's nearly an hour ago. I wondered then where her mother was. Where's your mum, love?' she said to the child.

The little girl suddenly wet her pants and simultaneously began to cry.

'Who're you waiting for?' asked the woman's husband.

But she just cried, quite silently, and looked down at the wetness spreading around her, and cried some more.

'We can't just leave her here,' said the woman.

A crowd had begun to gather.

'The police station's just round the corner,' said a bloke in a check cap. 'Why doncher slip over there and see if they've got any ideas? Someone's prob'ly lookin' for her.'

'Yeah, go on love!' said the woman.

But the young good-looking policeman, self-conscious in his high hard helmet and his uniform so new that the creases had hardly shaken out, who came in response to the husband's inquiry, said no-one had reported her missing.

'Where's your mum?' he asked the child.

'She doesn't talk,' said one of the bystanders. 'We can't get anything out of her.'

'Dumb, prob'ly,' said another.

'Yeah, deaf and dumb,' nodded a third.

'Better come round the station with me,' said the policeman, 'and we'll see if we can get you home.'

At the word 'home' she took the proffered hand and trotted beside him to the police station.

Only when she got there, it wasn't a station at all — only a sort of house. There were no trains.

There was another policeman there, red-faced, who fired a lot of questions at her:

'What's your name?'

'How old are you?'

'Where do you live?'

'Who did you come with?'

'Why don't you answer me?'

To all his questions she said nothing. She had stopped crying, and apart from twisting her body a little from side to side and staring, made no sign at all that she heard him. He rubbed his hands in perplexity across the stubble on his chin, making a rasping noise that reminded her of her father.

He took the young policeman aside and said something in his ear, and they went away for a moment. When the younger man returned, he sat down beside her and offered her a glass of milk and an iced cake. She drank the milk greedily and ate the cake, wiping cake crumbs and milk off her face with the back of her hand.

'What a pretty dress you've got on,' he said, and was amazed when she said simply: 'It's my best dress. I only wear it when I go out.' And she began to talk.

She lived in Deepdene, she said, and you could go there in the train. There was a *real* station there.

'We've got a house with stairs,' she said importantly. 'And there's a tram there, too, and a shop on the corner where Daddy buys the paper. And we've got chooks, and they lay brown eggs, and I have one in an eggcup for tea sometimes. And there's a house there for the pigeons.'

She told him about Jennie, who was real big and went to school.

'One night,' she said, 'Jennie got out of bed in her nightie in the middle of the night and walked all the way down to Mrs Blessington's place in her sleep. When Mr Blessington came out she asked for a drink of water, and he brought her home.'

She told him how Jock had got a hiding because he played with the hose and got dirty after Mother had got him all clean to go to Grandma's. And how Daddy had taken her on his bicycle and left her outside the cake shop while he went to buy something. And how she got frightened and wet her pants. She interrupted herself, and after a long pause she said quickly: 'I'm a big girl now, I'm three, and I *never* wet my pants,' and she smoothed her dress over the offending garment.

'No, I'm sure you don't,' said the policeman quickly.

She told him how Daddy worked for the electric, and how Uncle had bought her a doll with eyes that opened and shut and real hair, and Jennie said that it should have been hers, because she was the eldest.

'But Uncle doesn't come any more,' she said, and fell silent again.

The big red-faced policeman came back, with his policeman's hat on.

'Find anything out?' he asked.

'Don't know her name, but she comes from Deepdene, in a two-storey house near the station, and there's a tramline and a newsagent nearby.'

'Well, she can't stay here. Better take her to Deepdene. Sounds as if she might be able to find it herself, like, when she gets there. We can't keep her here, and it'd save a lot of trouble.'

'Where's Deepdene?'

'Near Kew, Hawthorn, out that way, on the outer circle railway line. Little steam train called the Deepdene Dasher.'

So she and the policeman went up the ramp to the Richmond station, a real one this time, and at last onto the little train to Deepdene. In the train the policeman took off his hard hat, and put it beside him on the seat, and she began talking again.

She told him about the baby, how he was always sick, and cried all the time, and Daddy didn't like people to cry –

She stopped and looked at her nice policeman, who had given her the cake and the drink of milk.

'I don't ever cry,' she said.

'No, I'm sure you don't,' he said again.

After a pause, she went off on another tack.

'Nick's my friend,' she said. 'That's short for Nicodemus,' getting her tongue round the word with no trouble at all.

'Dumb, is she?' thought the policeman.

'When we first got Nick,' she said, 'he was only a little puppy, and Daddy cut off his tail with the axe, and he squealed and squealed.'

After another long pause, she said quietly: 'Daddy put a pillow on the baby's face and he stopped crying, and they put him in the garden under the bean plants. Jennie said he'd died and gone to Heaven, but we can't go and see him — it must be too far.'

The train drew into Deepdene station, and she stopped talking and just walked beside him. He knew that she was taking him home, and not the other way round. She took him down a couple of streets and down a cobbled right-of-way and they went through the back gate of a house.

Yes! He felt a stab of recognition. It was two storey, so there were stairs, and there was the chookhouse and a pigeon-loft, and a ginger dog, presumably called Nick, who bounded forward, barking ferociously at the policeman, but stopped and wagged his stump of a tail as he saw the little girl.

Before he even knocked at the door it was opened by a small dark-haired woman of extraordinary beauty, who started when she saw them, and said sternly to the child: 'Where have you been? Your father is out looking for you!'

The young policeman, under the spell of the woman's beauty, began babbling, how the little girl had been standing on the corner at Richmond for so long that people had noticed and had sent for him.

'I knew as soon as I got here I had come to the right place, because she told me about the stairs, and about the chooks, and about the pigeons and the dog Nicodemus —'

He suddenly stopped as his gaze wandered past the silver beet to the bean patch.

The woman fastened her great eyes on him, and said gently: 'Yes? And what else did she tell you?'

Diffident now, and halting, and loosening his collar a little, he said: 'Well, she said . . . she said . . . she told me you had a baby buried under the bean plants!'

He began to giggle a little self-consciously.

The woman laughed, too.

'She's got the greatest imagination,' she said. 'We can never believe a word she says. The baby's gone to stay with his Grandmother, because I've not been well, and the kids were getting me down. She went out of the house this morning, by herself, before we were up, and it was a long time before we even missed her. Thank you very much for bringing her home. We're going to have to lock the doors every night in future.'

The policeman went away, almost backing out, so he could keep the image of her beautiful smiling face a little longer.

The child was left alone with her mother.

SCENE IN THE MORGUE

IT WAS 8 a.m. on a Saturday.

Ellie Peters was on her way to breakfast down the long dark corridor between the ward she had just left and the dining hall. She had been on duty since 6 a.m., and this was the last day of her six-day seventy-six-hour week. She hated that long gloomy corridor, illuminated by a single bulb dangling by its cord which disappeared, when it reached the wooden ceiling, into a length of black conduit across the ceiling and down the wall. But nothing, she felt, could darken her spirits at the prospect of breakfast now and a whole day off tomorrow.

A cry from below — she thought from the morgue — caused her to stop and turn back. George, one of the hospital porters who doubled as morgue attendant, stood at the top of the steps bellowing after her: 'Get a doctor, quick!'

'M-m-me?' she stammered, appalled at the prospect of tackling a god-like being, either doctor or sister.

'One of them's alive,' said George. 'She spoke to me. Get a doctor, quick as you can!'

And as she stood there not moving with her mouth open: 'Get a doctor, you bloody fool of a girl,' he bellowed.

She fled back to the ward.

'It's George!' she gulped, as she skidded to a halt at the sister's desk. 'He wants a doctor, quick!'

'George?' snapped the sister, trained to recognise an emergency when she saw one. 'What George? Pull yourself together, Nurse!'

The word 'nurse' did it.

'Nurse' she was not.

She was an underpaid, overworked, almost totally untrained 'Nurse-trainee', barely fifteen years old, who had been at the hospital just under three months, but long enough to jump to it when sister spoke.

'Yes, Sister. It's George, Sister. From the morgue. He says one of them's alive. It spoke to him. He wants a doctor down there, quick.'

Sister stared for a moment, no more, then she moved to the wall, lifted the earphone off the hook, wound the handle and spoke into the mouthpiece.

'Doctor Bradshaw?' she said. 'Sister James, from ward six. George from the morgue wants a doctor down there, quick. Says one of his corpses is talking back.'

She laughed.

'Well, he's convinced, anyway. He's grabbed one of my nurses on the way to her breakfast and frightened the wits out of her.'

She hung up and sent Ellie tottering off to get her breakfast.

Doctor Bradshaw went down to see George, intrigued, but not convinced.

'What's all this, George?' he asked.

'One of them spoke to me,' said George doggedly.

George had been at the hospital longer than Bradshaw, who was in the second year of his residency. Bradshaw knew him as little as anyone in this chaotic place knew anyone else from other ranks. He made no demands, asked no questions, rarely spoke except to the other porter. Since the appalling death rates from the influenza epidemic last year his job wasn't even up for jokes — it was something below stairs, and everybody liked it to stay that way.

Nobody but George went down to his windowless dark cellar, except by chute, and those who went by this route were not interested in the grating above for ventilation or the grating below for drainage, in the dimly shining light bulb, or the narrow, somewhat slimy steps that led to the corridor above. Only George went out by those steps; all the others who went into the morgue went out by a narrow door in the wall, horizontally.

Bradshaw saw that George at least believed what he was saying.

'Which one?'

'That kid with all the damage,' he said.

'She'll never speak again, from what I hear,' said Bradshaw decisively. 'Dr Llewellyn says her mouth and jaw were too damaged to function even if she were alive.'

'Not ... not that kind of talking,' said George hesitantly.

'No sounds. But I heard the words. She said: "Get me down."'

He didn't like what he was saying. He was a decent hard-working man who until today seemed to do his two jobs without being upset by any of the sights he saw. He had calmed down at the arrival of Bradshaw, but he shrank from saying what he felt he must say now.

'Not words,' he said again.

Bradshaw waited.

'Not words, like. Not out loud. But she said it into my head.'

His words began to come out in a rush.

'She said it twice. "Get me down," she said. She was on the floor when I come in this morning. That old codger, too,' pointing to another bag hanging from a hook. 'I fixed him up first. When I seen her, I reckoned it'd be easier to get him out of the way first. Then' — he squirmed a bit — 'I put her on the floor and hosed her down. She was such a mess! And I put her in a bag like always and hung it up. Then, as I was sweeping the water away, she spoke to me.'

'All right,' said Bradshaw, with reluctance. 'I suppose we'd better get her down and have a look at her.'

His reluctance was well founded. He'd been awakened at 2 a.m. the night before by the other resident, Lewis Llewellyn, who'd just come up from casualty.

'Jesus, John! Where's the whisky?' he'd said, as he shook him awake. After he'd found the bottle and gulped down a good half-glass, he'd repeated: 'Jesus! This kid came in, wrapped in a bit of old blanket. Shit! When I opened it up — you never saw anything like it in your life. What a mess! Someone had carved her up. And the stink! And she stank of brandy, too. I asked Joe — he'd brought her in, in the ambulance — who's been giving her brandy?

'Joe said it was the doctor back at the house. He thought she was dead at first, but then he'd given her brandy, and reckoned he got a heartbeat. But she was good and dead by the time I saw her. Dead and cold and stiff. The local must have imagined it when he thought he got a heartbeat. And thank God she was dead! I was glad I didn't have to start on her!'

He slurped down the second half of the whisky and stood for a moment.

'Jesus!' he said, 'You should have seen her! She was four years old! Joe reckoned they'd told him it was her fourth birthday. What a birthday present!'

Bradshaw had been wide awake by then. Rather astonished, he'd watched Llewellyn down his second large whisky.

They'd both seen some pretty bad sights in the last eighteen months in casualty, but he'd never before seen Llewellyn as anything but unflappable, almost to the point of cynicism.

So now he braced himself for the sight before he saw it.

When they slid the body out of the bag onto the trolley that stood by the wall, and Bradshaw looked at it, it was just as Llewellyn had described it, except that it didn't stink any more.

He put a stethoscope to her chest, and after a second he thought he heard a faint irregular rasping beat. He was almost able to convince himself that he didn't hear it.

He backed off a pace. He pointed to the damaged face, jaw, mouth, and said to George: 'You say she spoke?'

George nodded.

Bradshaw put the stethoscope back on her chest. Compared to the rest of her it was little damaged. One stab wound was right above the heart, but if there had been a heartbeat, the wound must have been very shallow or the knife deflected in some way. And as Bradshaw looked at it, he saw with horror that an almost imperceptible colouring of blood had begun to seep from it.

He put the stethoscope back to her chest and there it was again — a faint irregular rasping beat — was it stronger this time? He did not know, but he did know it was there.

He realised with dismay that he had to make a decision — and then he thought, no, perhaps he didn't; she had already made it for him when she 'spoke' to George.

'She's alive,' he said, and as he said it he realised they both breathed easier in the knowledge that it wasn't a ghost that had spoken, but a four-year-old girl asserting her right to live.

'But, God!' he said to himself, 'I'm going to have to do something about this. And whatever I do won't be enough. She'll die anyway!'

And then he heard her himself, where George had said he'd heard her — in his head.

'I won't die,' she said. 'I won't!'

PART ONE

CRY-BABY

WE ARE going to Auntie's. Hurrah! Hurrah! Hurrah!

Auntie is lovely. She used to be a piano teacher, but she has sore hands and she can't teach any more. She and Uncle Fred have a lolly shop in Bridge Road now.

When we get off the train, we have to cross the road, and the train goes roaring and rattling over our heads, even over Auntie's shop. What if it fell through, like the plaster rose that fell through from the ceiling onto my bed last week, just missing my toes? But soon we are safely inside, all on our best behaviour. It's easy to be on your best behaviour when you've got your best clothes on and there are other people there, and the grown-ups are not fighting.

First we are allowed to go into the shop and choose three lollies each, first Jock, then Jennie, then me. I choose a black liquorice baby, a sucker-on-a-stick and a sherbet-bag. Mother and Auntie go out to the kitchen to talk and laugh as they get dinner, while Daddy and Uncle Fred drink beer and lark around in the dining room. We are sent out to play, and Auntie's big boy Clem makes us play cricket in their little narrow back yard, a sort of passageway between two fences. Jennie is soon furious because they won't let her bowl or bat, only field.

'You're a girl!' they say indignantly.

She huffs off to the back of the shed to read the book she hid in her pants before we left home; Daddy and Mother are both inside enjoying themselves, so there is no-one to say: 'Put that book away!' or 'You'll go cross-eyed if your nose is always in a book!' or 'Haven't you got something better to do, when there's so much to be done?'

Now Jennie's gone it's my turn to field.

'Hey! Emma! Stop mooning around and throw the ball back to us!' But it is said without much conviction. I have been roped in to play cricket before, and am always much more interested in getting out of the way of that hard red ball than I am in catching or throwing it back.

'Butterfingers!' they yell.

'Catch it! Don't just stand there, you big sook!'

But they soon give up on me, and I am released to sneak up to the front parlour, forbidden territory in any house, and lift up the lid of the piano, and stroke the white bits, which make lovely sounds, each one different. I look up to see Auntie standing at the door, looking at me. I reach for the lid and wait for the inevitable: 'Don't touch!' or 'What do you mean by coming in here?'

But Auntie's eyes are shining.

'Do you like my piano?' she asks softly.

I nod warily.

'If you like, I could teach you to play it.'

And she does.

She wangles for me to stay with her for a week, though I haven't even brought a change of clothes.

'I'll find something for her to wear,' she says over Mother's feeble objections.

I sleep with Auntie (Uncle Fred sleeps in the back bedroom by himself) in the big squashy bed in her bedroom, which is dark and untidy; there are clothes and shoes on the floor, and the wardrobe door is hanging open. In the bottom drawer of the wardrobe there are lots of hats, and I am allowed to try them all on and make faces at myself in the mirror, while Auntie lies in bed reading the paper. The drawers of the dressing table are never closed, either, and she lets me rummage in them, in a mess of riches of touch and sight and smell such as I have never even dreamt of. In the top drawer are brushes and manicure scissors and files and emery boards and bottles of perfume and creams and lotions and powder puffs and spilt face powder — even a red lipstick, though I have never seen Auntie or anyone else wearing it.

The second drawer is full of white lace hankies and coloured ones, little bags of lavender with satin bows, diamanté and marcasite clips, combs of all sizes and shapes, a gold brooch with a horseshoe of diamonds in the centre, a jet necklace and an amber one tangled up with broken lengths of tiny red beads.

Auntie gives me a little bottle of scent and shows me how to put it behind my ears. 'That's so it's not too strong, and it wafts all round you and makes you smell lovely.'

At breakfast time, dressed in an old cardigan of Auntie's to save my dress, I creep under the table, lift up a lid and reach down among the spider webs into a little square hole under the table, called the cellar, from which I pass up the butter and the milk that have been kept cool there for the night.

After breakfast the real magic begins. Auntie starts doing what she does best and what she likes best, and teaches me to play the piano. I don't know how many hours we spend at it, but it is never enough. I am transported from the joyless, toyless world of home, where children must be seen and not heard, into another world in which it is not all *my fault,* and in which I am not difficult or scared or contrary. Soon I can recognise every note she plays. I have perfect pitch. I am a genius. I am encouraged, praised, admired, successful. I blossom. I thrive.

Auntie's hands are already becoming crippled with arthritis, so she gives me her piano and comes every week to give me a lesson. She tells Mother and Daddy that I have great talent. It is not a word I know, but it is praise. I haven't met praise before and it is heady stuff.

I now have the piano at home all the time, and I can go and play with it whenever I like — practise over and over the things like little games that Auntie has shown me, so I can do them perfectly.

There are rumblings from Daddy.

'Precocious little brat! I'm not having her do anything better than me!'

And the piano annoys him.

'Fancy giving an expensive present like that to a kid her age!'

Finally he says to Mother: 'You'll have to shut that kid up! She's driving me mad! I can't bear to hear her banging away on those scales!'

He has painful memories of learning piano himself from Auntie, his much older sister, when he was little.

'She'll make your life a misery!' he says darkly to me. 'When I was little, she would tell that little china man, who still sits in the armchair on Grandmother's mantelpiece, to watch me when I did my practice, and if I didn't do it properly, he'd tell her, and she'd hit me with the ruler.'

Mother too is enraged at me getting way into Auntie's good graces and being singled out for her favours.

'You should never have been up in the front room in the first place, worming your way into people's affections!! There's more to be considered in this house than you, my girl!'

So they sell the piano and buy a pianola. There are some good times, with me sitting on Daddy's lap as he pedals and sings the songs. The words, he says, are written on the roll under the notes, but the pianola sounds quite different from the piano. My own legs are not long enough to reach the pedals so I can't make the music myself, and I am frightened of the magic: that Daddy could put a roll in and those little holes in the paper would make it play tunes, and the keys would jump up and down as though someone I couldn't see were playing it. What with that, and the little old china man being able to tell on Daddy, it almost seems as if the magic of the fairy stories could be true, and perhaps people really could put a spell on you. Auntie and her piano have suddenly become very scary. When she comes back next week for her lesson, everything is changed. I don't run to meet her but hang back, and she stands looking at the cheap veneer pianola standing where her old fiddleback walnut piano had stood. She is quite pale.

'You've sold my piano!' she says.

Nobody else says anything at all. Mother shoos her out to the kitchen and starts chattering and clattering as she gets the tea. Nobody mentions the piano or the lessons again.

If I fail Auntie as her infant prodigy, later she fails me, as we all fail each other in our expectations of perfect love. I go again to stay with her, this time with Jennie and Jock, in a vast dark old mansion in St Kilda Road, belonging to some very important people, where she is working as a caretaker. There is a little frame on the wall in the big cold kitchen, and if you pull on a tasselled rope in one of the grand rooms upstairs, a light shines in the little frame to tell the maids where to go. There are no maids now, and we have fun running from room to room pulling the ropes.

At night we three sleep together in a huge bed with curtains all round it, but in the middle of the night I wake up screaming: 'They're killing the baby! They're killing the baby!'

I can't be comforted or consoled until Auntie, distraught, says 'I'll have to send for your father, if you don't stop!' She gives me brandy, which takes my breath away. Between the brandy and the threat, I am silenced. We don't go home for a week, and when we do, we learn that my baby brother, Ronald George, has died.

'Died?'

'Gone away.'

'Where to?'

'To a better place. He's with God.'

God I do not know, except as someone Grandmother seems to know, and as an ally of Mother's who will strike me dead if I tell lies or answer back. I cannot be comforted. For a while I can't stop crying. I cry and cry, until I have nearly forgotten what I am crying about. News of my carryings-on at Auntie's have got home to Mother, and I am not to be trusted out of their sight again.

My crying drives Mother mad.

'If you don't stop crying, I'll have to send you back to the hospital where you came from,' she says in desperation.

Daddy takes me away to the bedroom and stands me on the po-cupboard, so that his face is very close to mine.

'*There was no baby*,' he says softly. 'You dreamt it all. Don't ever let me see you crying again!'

And in my whole life I never do.

GRANDMOTHER

MOTHER IS up unusually early. She puts a clean nightie on me and washes my face, brushes my short spiky hair, and sits me, dangling precariously, on a chair at the porch door while she and Jock drag the shaky wicker couch off the back veranda into the yard.

'Not in the sun! Here under the plum tree! She's been inside so long she'll burn to a crisp if the sun gets to her!'

Mother even speaks to me directly as she tucks the rug carefully round my legs.

'We don't want anyone to see those legs, do we?'

But what about the face, Mother?

Auntie Doll is coming to lunch. Jock has been allowed to stay home from school. He is in his best clothes, with his socks pulled up instead of fallen down onto the tops of his boots, and he has whispered it to me under a vow of secrecy, but I know it anyway. There has been such a flurry of cleaning, scrubbing of draining boards and table tops, mopping of floors, polishing of boards, blackening of fireplaces, pitching of things into wardrobes, smoothing of quilts, ironing of tablecloths, and flowers — flowers! — on the table, that I know someone is coming, and the only one who ever comes nowadays is Auntie.

Mother comes out again, brush in hand doing her hair, to hiss in Jock's ear: 'Don't tell Emma. You know what she is! If she gets upset, she'll say anything that comes into her head, and Doll may not be able to get away.'

Too late, Mother, the cat's already out of the bag!

Doll is Auntie, Auntie of my piano days, when I was cast as her child prodigy. She is Auntie of the lolly shop in Bridge Road, where she used to live with Uncle Fred and her big boy Clem. She is Auntie of the little china man sitting on Grandmother's mantelpiece, who used to tell on Daddy if he hadn't done his music practice. She is Auntie of the big house she was caretaker of, where she said to me: 'If you don't stop crying, I'll have to send for your father!'

But all these Aunties fade, because today she will be Auntie-at-home-alone-with-Mother, and in her company Mother stops being I'm-your-mother-and-you-won't-best-me and starts talking and laughing and acting as though she likes us, and doesn't even notice if we don't eat everything on our plates, or if we accidentally spill something on the cloth.

So I lie outside for the first time since I fell down the stairs (*Cover up those legs or they'll know she didn't fall down the stairs!*) with little wibbly-wobbly bits of sunlight streaming down on me through the leaves of the plum-tree, where there are birds singing as they try to find some ripe bits on the half-green plums, and the pigeons in the pigeon-loft are making coo-coo noises as though there were no such thing as pigeon pie, and I forget about my face because I am the same inside and because it is a beautiful morning and because it is wonderful to be outside again after so long, and because Auntie is coming and I am happy.

The sun gets higher and hotter. I doze off and wake to Mother bursting out, angry because it is so late that she knows Doll won't be coming, and it has all been for nothing. She gets ready to shunt me inside and I begin to bawl because I'm sure I'll never see Auntie again, and Mother shouts at me: 'I'll never let you outside again!' and then at Jock: 'You told her! you little devil! I told you not to tell!' She keeps clipping him round the ears till he manages to get out of her reach, and he is bawling too.

Later, back in the bedroom, Jock comes in to hiss at me: 'You told her! You told her! I'll never tell you anything again!'

Auntie hasn't come on her own for a long time now. Uncle Fred is another one who has just disappeared and is not to be mentioned. They have left the lolly shop in Richmond and Auntie has moved in with Grandmother. But she still has her bag, a big deep black one, in which we are still allowed to fish for pink and white striped candy walking sticks, or toffee lamp-posts on a stick, or little bags of jelly beans or boiled lollies. Sometimes there are even marbles for Jock, or a spinning top or a hair ribbon for me. It is not the same, though, because when she comes now, Grandmother always comes too.

Grandmother is Daddy's 'Ma' or 'The Old Girl' or 'The Old Lady', and she is not like anyone else I know. She lives with Grandfather in a lovely little house near the sea in Sandringham. She is very old and fat and lumpy, with white hair and little brown-black eyes that see everything. She always wears black. She comes from Ireland.

I pick up bits of information about her from Mother when Grandmother is not about. 'Irish!' says Mother.

'Bog Irish,' says Mother.

'Beyond the pale!' says Mother.

These remarks are not addressed to me, or anyone else. Mother rips them out before Grandmother comes, as she scrubs the white boards of the kitchen table with a vigour close to violence, and I take them in and digest them, along with all the other indigestible stuff, as best I can.

'Turned white overnight!' says Mother in conversation this time with Auntie Jean. 'And no wonder!' And they exchange meaningful glances, and shake their heads, but there is no explanation of what made Grandmother's hair turn white overnight.

In spite of all the undercurrents, it is still treat time when they come and, kisses on the cheek over, we fish for treasure in Auntie's bag, and Mother leaves Grandmother in the bedroom to change while she and Doll hurry outside for a few private words on the awfulness of having to live with Grandmother. (Mother had done a stint when Jennie was a baby, while Daddy was away at the war.)

Sucking on my walking stick, I am left alone with Grandmother while she unwraps herself, unwinds her shawl, and takes off her coat and her black straw hat. Before the hat can come off, she has to unscrew the end of the long hat-pin that skewers her hat onto her hair.

'I wear this everywhere I go,' she says to me low in the bedroom. 'It's as good as a dagger if anyone tries any funny business.'

I am jolted.

It is this that makes Grandmother so different from anyone else. She says things no-one else would say, straight at you, as though you were not just a child to be corrected or ignored, but someone who mattered.

She tells us stories that make Mother roll her eyes heavenwards, but Grandmother just goes on without ever seeming to notice. She actually interrupts Mother sometimes as she explains something like what 'beyond the pale' means. It means in the olden days living outside the fence around the village that protected people from the barbarians. In Ireland, it means a sort of fence thing made of rocks that separated the good Irish, like Grandmother who is Protestant, from the bad Irish, who are Catholics. At this time we are living in a street of new houses, all without fences, so I am not sure whether we are barbarians or Protestants. I know we are not Catholics, which is the worst thing to be.

She tells us one story we all love about the time her mother sent her down to the market to buy a rock melon. I have never seen a rock melon and have trouble picturing it. She has told us this story often before, but none of us except Mother ever get tired of it.

'When I got home with the melon,' says Grandmother, and the little shoe-button eyes begin to sparkle, 'Ma took the melon, and said: "Will you take a look at that, will you? It's rotten, it is! Take it back to him! I'm not paying for any rotten melon."

'So I took it back,' says Grandmother, 'but the man wouldn't give me my money back.

'But,' says Grandmother, 'I gave him a power of cheek' — and by this time she is doubling up and clutching her sides and laughing so much that the tears are squeezing out of her eyes, and she is gasping for air — 'and I says to him: "Yes, you will take it back!" and I throw it at him and I run for my life!'

And I see the man in the market with the melon running down his face and his apron, and though I am scared I am laughing with Grandmother, and full of admiration for her daring deed.

Another time while Mother is getting the tea, Grandmother tells us about coming out on a ship from Ireland. 'Big waves, some as high as a house, and the sea and the sky as black as your hat all around, and everybody huddled together and frightened out of our wits.

'In the daytime, when it was calm, it was different, but there was little to do except keep watch for another ship in the distance, which might take letters home to Ireland to Grannie, who was minding my little brother and sister until Ma and Da could send for them. Sometimes men dropped little boats over the side into the water and went fishing from them, some even swam, but mostly they were too frightened of the sharks.

'There was a time when there was a great hullabaloo, and a shout "Man overboard!" The crew rushed about with ropes and held out lights over the side.

'There was no sign of the man, and the sea was too wild to lower a boat down. They said the sharks would have him before morning. Some said he jumped because he couldn't stand being on the ship any more, but whatever, he was gone, and there was an end of it!

'Glad it was we all were to land in Melbourne, though at first I thought we must have come to the wrong place, it was so cold and poor-looking. Back in Ireland we'd heard tales about long days full of sunshine, and ships full of gold coming to England from Australia, where you could just dig it up out of the street, but if they had all this gold, why did they send it all away, instead of buying some nice houses and better things for themselves? I could see no sign of either the sunshine or the gold.

'At first when we got off the ship, my legs wouldn't hold me up properly, and I was staggering all over the place. There were so many people there, all talking and laughing and excited to see each other, but the Maloneys — they'd come before us and said they'd meet us here — weren't there. Perhaps they'd fallen overboard too, or been thrown overboard, like some from down below on the ship who'd got sick and died.

'We stayed for a few days at an inn near the ship, but it was not like the inn near where we lived at Tipperary. There was so much noise and shouting and fighting that my brother and I had to stay up in the room with Ma, while Da went out and talked to people to find out what best to do and where best to go. In the end, they put all our things in a dray and we went down the St Kilda Road and on to a little quiet beach called Sandringham, and lived in a tent with lots of other Irish people. After all the time being shut up on the ship or at the inn, it was lovely to be able to run around again.

'My Ma said we went wild.'

I've seen Grandmother talk like this to Daddy: her voice goes on and on in a long low murmur, almost like the sea itself. When Grandmother is wound up she can talk for ever. 'Nails you!' says Mother. 'Well, she won't nail me!' So too soon Mother comes out with her what's-going-on-here look on her face, and says dinner's ready, and we all go out to the kitchen to eat.

Even at the table Grandmother keeps talking, and Mother doesn't say to her: 'No talking at the table!'

Jock takes advantage of this to ask: 'What do those big letters on your case mean, Grandmother?'

She has a little brown cardboard case that she takes everywhere with her, though I have never seen it opened. On it in big black letters it says: AWNLand Grandmother, laughing, says it means: ANNIE WILTSHIRE, NO LADY. The letters really stand for AUSTRALIAN WOMEN'S NATIONAL LEAGUE, of which Grandmother is a founding member.

'Not foundling,' she says, laughing again in answer to Jock's question. 'It's founding! It means I helped to start it!'

When she has gone, Daddy snorts. 'Australian Women's National League! Politics! What next? Women! Why can't they keep their noses out of things that don't concern them!' But while she is there, he seems to be drinking in her words like everybody else.

Another time she starts telling us about the black men — Aborigines, they are called — who had a camp — a group of little houses, each one shaped like a spinning top upside down, with no windows or doors, where they all lived. It was round the point at Sandringham from where the Irish were, and once — and as she talks I begin to see little-girl Grandmother, a little girl with long black hair and the same shoe-button eyes, wearing a long bedraggled dress with raggy ribbons hanging from it. She is with a black man, a man with no clothes on except something over his thing, and he is taking her along the beach to show her the camp where the black people live. He says he will show her how they catch fish, but the other black people are angry with him, and start talking and shouting and waving their arms, and pointing up the beach to where they have come from, and they go back towards her own people.

'We went along the beach a-ways,' says Grandmother, 'till we came to some caves in the cliff, and we went in.'

Grandmother looks at me, as I stand staring and drinking it all in, and she tails off and the black eyes become wary, and she says what the grown-ups always say when they see me listening so intently: 'Why don't you go out and play, while I have a talk with your mother?'

It is too late. I have seen what I am not supposed to see — I have seen Grandmother in the cave with the black man. Her dress is off — but I push it away. I have seen Grandmother once before when she got talking, and I know it is more than I can handle to see any more.

But in the night I have one of my dreams, one that I have had before, and I wake up sobbing, but very quietly, so no-one will hear.

Grandmother, in my dream, sits beside the well. It is very dark. She is unwrapping a bundle, a mewing bundle, with a blanket around it. She opens it, and picks up what is inside the blanket — it is a baby, not a kitten — holds it by the legs, and dashes its head against the side of the well.

'We wouldn't want her to suffer,' she says.

There is a little silence from the deep well, then the sound of a splash. Now I can see that there is a shadowy figure beside her at the well, which becomes little-boy Daddy, his eyes bigger than they are now. He is dressed in a little suit with a big white collar. Together they cover the top of the well with a bit of old iron nailed to some boards, and there is ivy growing all over it, and it becomes the top of the old well that I remember in the fenced-off bit of Grandmother's backyard when she lived in Brunswick.

It is good to wake up!

Sometimes, to give Mother a spell, I am invited to go and stay at Grandmother's Victorian house near Sandringham. It has a little front yard with no lawn, only flower beds in straight lines, and no matter when you go there are always flowers blooming — pink ones and blue ones and yellow ones, and in spring a big bush of white may. Inside the house is dark, with a long dark dangerous passage down the middle, but the sitting room has big windows and is light and warm, with a little fire always burning in the grate surrounded by the green tiles with the yellow flowers on them. There is a book cupboard with glass doors, and in between *Holy Bible* and Josephus' *History of the Jews* there is a square jar of extra special boiled lollies with hard outsides and mushy insides, and as soon as we get there, she gives us one each, and we suck on it while the grown-ups talk, and we feel WELCOME, like the mat at the front door says.

There is a squeaky rocking chair there, too, that I remember from always. It has a sort of carpet seat that prickles your bottom even through your pants.

When I stay there, I sleep on a wobbly bed under the eiderdown in the sleep-out, a boarded-up bit of the veranda that runs around the house. I can hear the roar of the sea in the distance. One night the rain beats so loudly on the scalloped tin roof, and the sea crashes so wild in the distance and the wind shrieks through the wire door and rattles it so hard, that I run barefooted in terror in my nightie along the veranda to bang on the big oak front door, screaming to be let in, let in, and Grandmother comes to the door in her nightie, with her little eyes popping, and her scraggy white hair all down around her like the witch in *Hansel and Gretel*, and she takes me in and is kind.

She wraps me in a rug, and gives me a drink of warm milk with brandy and sugar in it, and sits in the rocking chair with me and my rug and my drink all cradled in her arms. She makes crooning noises like the sea when it is quiet, and cuddles me.

'I've rocked all my children to sleep in that chair,' she says. I think of what I saw — that I kept dreaming about — the baby in the well, and I silently ask: 'All except one, Grandmother?'

I think Daddy was wrong when he said no-one could ever love me again.

SCOTTISH NEW YEAR

'HAPPY NEW Year!' says my father in festive mood when we get to Grandma's.

'Happy 1924!'

He is Grandma's 'first footer', the first person to cross the threshold on New Year's day; if he is a tall dark man, according to the Scottish custom, he will bring good luck for the whole year.

Grandma is my mother's mother, and sometimes when she is looking stern her face looks just like Mother's, only old. Daddy is both tall and dark, and as he walks in, Grandma's strong, stern face relaxes into beauty as she smiles and puts her face up to be kissed.

Daddy has that effect on women.

Lately, I am allowed to go to Grandma's with everybody else.

I go down the passage, hang my little Christmas stocking handbag on the brass knob of Grandma's dining-room door, and for the first time I am conscious of time: it is 1924. I am five years old. I am a big girl.

The big table in the dining room still has its green velvet cover with the fringes tied in knots all round, so dinner won't be ready for a while, but the smell of it makes my mouth water — chooks and roast potatoes! I somehow don't want to associate these chooks with the chooks in the pen at the bottom of the garden, though I know such things happen: we had pigeons once — but I shut that down, too.

Grandpa's sitting on the couch, with earphones on his ears from the crystal set. He does not look up as we walk in.

Jock has explained to me about the crystal set and how it works. He is a genius in such matters. Many's the hiding he's had for taking the lock off the door, or taking to pieces the donkey-engine or the clock to find out how they work. So far he is better at taking them apart than he is at putting them back together again.

Once we have an iron moneybox in the shape of a dog. You put threepence on his tongue and pull his tail, and the threepence goes inside him. Jock soon discovers that he can unscrew a round bit underneath the dog and get the money out. We start taking the threepences to Mr Furlonger's shop on the corner and he gives us lollies for them. It's lovely!

Mother finds out, and when Daddy comes home late on Saturday night she must have told him. On Sunday morning — often a time for reckonings — we are summoned into the bedroom and Daddy starts roaring and yelling, and calls Jock a thief, and leaps out of bed ready to wallop him. Suddenly, to everybody's amazement, I break a long silence and begin to roar, too.

'He's not a thief!' I yell. 'It was his money in the dog! You gave it to him and me for pocket money! So it wasn't stealing!'

Daddy stops, and his eyes go red. All he says is: 'Right. I'm not having anyone answer me back in my own house! It's off to the Burwood Boys' Home with both of you!'

He bundles us into the front seat of the car and starts to drive out, with Mother standing on the running board saying: 'Now, calm down, Rex! Calm down!' but she has a sort of smile on her face and I can sense that in some way she is enjoying it all. Whether she got off or fell off, I don't know.

At the wide entrance to the great big house, where the hoarding out the front says: BURWOOD BOYS' HOME, for no reason that I can see Daddy suddenly turns the car around, with a squeal of tyres, and begins to head for home. I don't know whether to be glad or sorry — anywhere would be better than home, I think. I don't know what made him turn around. Is it because I thought: 'I will never answer anyone back again?' Is it because I am a girl, so they wouldn't take me in the boys' home?

I only remember the drive home, and my wonder at the amazing way the steep black ribbon of road flattened out as we sped down the long hill towards the crossroad with the tram-tracks on it that led to home.

Jock still takes things to pieces, harder things than the dog moneybox, but he's better now at putting them back together again. I can often make nothing of his explanations. It is because I am stupid. I know that it is true because I have been told so often, and because there are so many things I do not understand, and I am not only talking about things like the crystal set that Grandpa is listening to through the earphones.

Jock and I park down on the couch, 'out of the way', next to Grandpa.

The couch is hard, stuffed with horse-hair, and covered with harsh dry black leather, cracked and bald in patches from age and wear. Its back curves away to a beautiful piece of polished wood, ending in a wooden flower. It is sort-of nice — I don't yet know elegant — but its well-buttoned back slopes away so that no-one, however degenerate, could lean back or slouch or slump against it.

Grandma has a couple of wise sayings about couches: 'A couch in the kitchen is a woman's best friend,' and 'Never stand when you can sit, never sit when you can lie.'

I can't imagine anyone lying on this couch. Instead, I have a sudden memory of a near-naked skinny brown Indian from a picture book lying on a bed of nails.

And friend? Best friend?

Grandpa, perched on the end of the couch, seems to be doing a whole string of forbidden things: going into a dream, listening to things that don't concern him, ignoring those around him, and having 'that look' on his face that I was always being warned to get off mine.

Jock and I, feeling safely ignored, start squirming and whispering and giggling on the couch, and Grandpa comes out of his trance to bellow at us: '*Be quiet!* Can't you see that I'm listening to *the news*?'

Uncle Don arrives, with Auntie Jean. Uncle Don is Mother's dark-haired older brother. He likes me, he is always kind and gentle with me. Jock hates him, perhaps with good reason.

'Why can't you be more like your Uncle Don?' says Mother at regular intervals.

'Your Uncle Don is one of nature's gentlemen,' says Mother.

'If you're as good as your Uncle Don, you'll do!' says Mother.

Perhaps Uncle Don senses Jock's antagonism: he always finds something to criticise. He tries to make a man of him.

'Hasn't anyone told you that a gentleman takes his hat off in the house?'

The simple answer is no, nobody ever did, but Jock just glares and takes his cap off and stuffs it in his pocket. Such exchanges make me wary of Uncle Don, even though he is always so nice to me. In later life I learn from the classics to 'Beware of Greeks bearing gifts', but from my five years' experience, I have already learned that if someone is being extra nice to you, you had better look out.

Yet Uncle always invites me, and only me, to his house to stay with him and his two women. I don't know why he is allowed to have two women. There used to be an old man there who was blind, with dark glasses and a stick, but he has long since done the disappearing act.

Auntie Jean is the mother, though she has no children.

'Poor Jean! She has no children of her own. That's why I let Emma stay with them so much,' says Mother, when Auntie Jean goes out to pick parsley and mint for the sauces.

'Poor Jane!' says Grandma of Mother, when she goes out to turn the vegetables. 'All those children!'

Auntie Jean is always very kind to me, but she says very little, except 'Time for dinner!' or 'Time for bed!' Once she bowls me out for pinching biscuits from the biscuit barrel.

'Not without asking,' she says, looking with exasperation, grief almost, first at the nearly empty barrel and then at me.

I squirm, but I don't say anything. She doesn't smack me or scream: 'Answer me!' or 'Look at me when I'm speaking!' or 'I'll give it to you!'; I don't know how to handle such restraint.

I suppose with Aunt Polly, Uncle's other lady, I *like* to look at her when she speaks. She is the only adult, except Daddy when he is in a good mood, who ever just chats to me, without trying to improve me.

She has — not a shop — a 'High Class Establishment',

whatever that is, in Howey Court, which is in town, where she makes dresses for ladies.

She tells me about her ladies.

'I measure them twice, always,' she says crossly, 'and when they come back in a week for a fitting, with some of them there's a difference of four or five inches! They go up and down like balloons!'

Aunt Polly brings me home big paper bags full of patches, scraps of bright colourful materials left over from her ladies' dresses. I dress peg dolls with them, and when I am at Uncle's, they leave me in peace for hours to play with them.

I wonder who wears the dresses made out of these gorgeous materials? Nobody I know.

My mother has two dresses in my mind-pictures of her. The first is her night-dress, a big blue flannelette one with pink roses on it and a blue bow at the neck, and in my picture of her, her long black lustrous hair is hanging down her back. The other dress is brown, buttoned high to the neck, with a rising star brooch on her breast, and her hair done up in a loose bun at the back. In both these pictures she is very beautiful.

But she has had short hair for a long time now, and I have no mind-picture of what she looks like now.

Uncle Don takes me to his shed, his secret place, where the women don't go. I am honoured. It has tools hanging all over the walls, and a bench with a top made of railway sleepers. (Uncle works for the railways, and I like to imagine him driving a massive snorting steam engine, but whatever he does in the railways, I know it is not that, because he does it in the workshops at Newport.)

On this bench-top Uncle hammers and bangs away at things; on it he makes me a kind of doll, with a big wooden bead for a head, and arms and legs made of strips of wood joined together with wire threaded through holes, so that the arms and legs move. He is very pleased with it.

I use coloured pencils to draw blue eyes and a red mouth on the bead, and I dress it in some of the gorgeous patches, but they do not suit it, and it has no heart, and its movements are stiff and jerky. It makes me sick to look at it. I go back to the peg dolls.

Later we lose touch with Uncle Don ('that sanctimonious bastard!').

When I am at university, I will remember the patches. I will spend 3/2d, a fortnight's spending money, on a ticket to the Russian Ballet. To get this bargain we have to get to Allan's Music House in Collins Street by 6.30 a.m. to get a coupon which we can redeem at 9 a.m. and be given a ticket. I think all this is to avoid any unseemly scramble in Collins Street when there are people about. In the meantime we go down to the banks of the Yarra and eat the breakfasts we have brought and sing bawdy songs in French and English. I feel very grown-up and bohemian.

The great night comes, my first visit to a live theatre.

I am up in the gods, on a hard seat, too excited to talk. Soon the lights go out, the music starts, the other students and the rest of the audience dissolve, and I am a child again, alone with the magic that is happening on stage.

Polly's patches are everywhere, exotic and expensive, bright and dark, velvets and silks, tinselled and spangled, ribboned and feathered, flared and gathered and tucked and pleated, and the music that I remember from another life is casting a spell on me, so that I am on stage too, dancing and leaping, swinging and swirling, and dressed in gorgeous patches, and flying, flying . . .

The scene on the stage changes, and the wooden doll with the bead head is there now, with bright red patches on her cheeks, dancing round in that jerky way that still makes me shudder.

Suddenly the curtains are drawn, the lights go on, the dancers bow from the stage, and we all flow back into our bodies again.

But all this is twelve, thirteen years away, and for the moment I am back in Grandma's dining room, where the meat has been lifted out of the oven, and delicious smells are wafting about. The big white damask cloth is now on the table, set with silver cutlery taken out of the box lined with green felt and polished up for the occasion, the great heavy leather-seated chairs with their carved backs have been dragged in on their castors from the sitting room and hallway and bedrooms, where they have sat out-of-the-way till needed. Pepper shakers and salt cellars are brought in, and mint sauce, (there is a leg of lamb as well as chooks) and the gravy boat and the bread-board with bread and the bread-knife on it. There is no butter. (I have not yet seen bread without butter, but it is used to mop up the gravy — scrumptious!)

There is little conversation except pass-the-salt or mind-your-manners; we all sit round and eat steadily, relishing the feast.

Grandpa is in a tearing hurry to finish, begrudging us even the time to hunt for threepences in the New Year pudding, or to scrape the last skerrick from our plates and eye the dish in the centre to see whether there'll be enough for seconds.

But at last we are all finished. We all rise together. The kids don't have to help with the dishes, because there are already four women who can barely squeeze into the kitchenette. The table is quickly cleared. Grandpa has disappeared up the front and he now emerges carrying a cribbage board and a bottle of whisky and two glasses, one for himself, one for Daddy. (Uncle Don, nature's gentleman, does not play or drink.)

During one of these cribbage games I have heard Daddy talking very confidentially to Grandpa, after a couple of whiskies.

'Blackened my reputation,' he is saying. 'Took away my good name and spread lies about me, in my own house, my own family.'

Smooth as silk his whisky-oiled voice goes on.

'You wouldn't believe the lies she told about me, as though it was gospel. My own flesh and blood! I only put up with it for the sake of my wife. And here's me slaving my guts out for the lot of them.'

Grandpa makes a few little noises between a chuckle and a cluck, Grandma comes out and takes the whisky bottle away, and I am shooed outside.

But on this New Year's Day Grandpa is already giggling, transformed into the blue-eyed rosy-cheeked jolly Santa Claus Grandpa with white whiskers and a curly pipe. Not a snarl, not a bellow; such things are entirely alien to this jovial fellow as he sucks the whisky through his stained moustache and tamps the tobacco down in his pipe.

The women by now exude an air of disapproval over the cards and the whisky.

'Now, Dad,' warns Grandma, 'don't get too silly.'

But the women begin to relax, too, as they wash up for twelve and prepare the food for tea: cold meat and a salad made up of chopped lettuce and a runny dressing and a pattern of sliced hard-boiled eggs and tomatoes on top.

'Go out and play!' they order us. They mean, I know, to go up the front bedroom and talk dark secret women's things: my mother's asthma, Auntie Aileen's many operations, what-I-said-to-the-doctor and what-the-doctor-said-to-me, how well Emma's doing at school, Andrew's beautiful drawings. Uncle Ed and that woman he's taken up with, and what happened to the last girl, the brunette, such a nice girl, but no! he has to go off with someone like this, and she is no better than she should be.

How good should she be? I wonder, not out loud, but they spot me listening in at the door and boot me out. Jock and I go off and chase the chooks, and though the rooster's pretty scary, they rush about and squawk in a most satisfying way until Uncle Don comes out and roars at Jock — not at me — for putting them off the lay.

We go out and give cheek to a couple of passing kids, knock the heads off a few daisies, and sneak out the front gate and into the next street where there is a big old house with an attic and a square turret surrounded by iron lace, where, Jock tells me, Bluebeard lives.

Gullible as I am, I can't quite swallow that one. That turret is not big enough for Bluebeard and sister Anne and the new wife and the guilty secrets too.

But I am scared enough to want to get back to Grandma's as quickly as possible.

When it is not Christmas holidays, I am sometimes invited to Grandma's while my cousins Annette and Veronica are there. They are not much older than me but very much bigger. They are built on Amazonian lines like their mother, Aunt (never Auntie) Margaret, a big statuesque beautiful woman with copper-coloured hair like her mother. She is the eldest of Grandma's children and my mother speaks of her with awe, because she left home before she got married, and got a job in the country. Not only did she display this undaughterly streak by leaving home too soon, but she also married a Catholic, Uncle Jack, who is a lawyer, and who is memorable for only one thing: he brews his own beer.

He doesn't tell us kids jokes, or pinch our cheeks, or correct our manners, or give us lollies, or do any of the things that uncles are supposed to do. I suspect he is rather nice, though a Catholic, which is known to be a pretty bad thing.

'Bloody Catholics!' roars Daddy at home, when he is not being convivial over Uncle Jack's home brew. 'They're taking over the place! Public service is riddled with them! Nobody else can get a look in!'

Beside Annette and Veronica I am a pigmy, but they are very chatty and agreeable and I feel quite friendly towards them. Neither they nor their parents seem aware of their Catholicism as a defect, and are not affected by the small hints and innuendoes dropped around them.

One Easter when I am staying at Grandma's, they take me to midnight mass. I am very glad that they are there, one either side of me. The church is an old stone one and bitterly cold, which always affects me badly. There are candles, and flickering shadows, and people with beads muttering in a fearful secret way (are they putting spells on someone?) and we are all bobbing down on our knees and up again, and the man up the front says something in a strange language, and we are supposed to say something back, but I don't know the words. Nobody notices, so I am not in trouble. But

Veronica and Annette start to giggle as my panic rises and I begin bobbing up and down not quite in sync with everybody else.

At last we put our threepences in the plate and escape, at least I escape — the other two do not seem awed by it at all.

Perhaps they even sense my distress, as they shepherd me kindly back through the frosty night to Grandma's. We all sleep in a great big double bed in a back bedroom, with me safely in the middle between the Amazons. No nightmares that night!

Beautiful blond blue-eyed Uncle Ed still lives at home. ('Twenty-eight! It's time he was married!' 'Poor Mum! She's got enough to do without looking after him! At her age!')

What is her age?

Although she has some wrinkles, her hair is still copper-brown and curly except for an interesting white streak on one side of her forehead, whereas I do not remember Grandpa as ever being anything but white-haired and white-whiskered. Grandma's complexion is still fine and fair and clear, but she is understood to be suffering from various unspecified and probably unmentionable complaints.

'We must look after Grandma; she won't be with us long.'

Is it wishful thinking?

I know we don't stay long in the house we bought in Brunswick so as to be near her, but then we don't stay long in any house.

'Couldn't wait to get a house near the old girl!' Daddy storms at the kitchen table to us children when Mother is out of the room, but not out of earshot. 'But couldn't get away quick enough when she did!'

'Don't touch that!' says Auntie Nell, Mother's youngest sister sharply, when we are staying at Grandma's while Mother is in hospital having 'a little operation'.

'That' is an infinitesimal pot of Marmite. It is full of a wonder substance called vitamins, just invented. ('You can't see them, stupid!') They make you strong and healthy; just a smear on your bread will put roses in your cheeks. I hate it because it is black and bitter, and that is just as well, because it is all for Grandma, to strengthen her tenuous grip on life. It must have worked; she was eighty-six when she died.

When Veronica and Annette and I stay there together, as usual we are sent out soon after breakfast, this time to cut up leek leaves for the chooks. Soon we are all streaming at the eyes, but I don't mind; at least I am included, and given a knife, and not considered too stupid. I expect very little of life, and know that I have only been invited to give poor Jane a spell. And the usual conditions apply. I am not to be a trouble to poor Grandma, and *no nonsense* (which I understand very well: it means no crying, and no leaking of family secrets).

In one of our games Veronica sends me to get some water from the wash-house, which with the lavatory is in a block separate from the house. A few days later Uncle Ed goes to the wash-house and finds that the curved steel troughs have rust all over them; they should have been thoroughly wiped and dried after use.

'Look what you've done to Grandma's troughs! You girls think you've got a staff of servants to clean up after you! You think you can come here and take over the place! Just wait till your father comes back!'

This, from Uncle Ed, is a serve in tone and body language so exactly like Mother that I am dumbfounded, and make no response at all.

Veronica and Annette have more gumption and defend themselves vigorously. Uncle Ed takes offence, and drags us before Grandma, who looks around vaguely and says 'Tsk! Tsk' several times, and sends us out to play.

When Aunt Margaret comes to pick up her daughters, they take her aside and tell her all about it. It amazes me that anyone would confess a transgression to their mother, and it amazes me still more when she makes soothing noises like: 'Grandma's getting old,' and 'Uncle Ed doesn't have any children, so he doesn't understand. There, there, don't worry about it.'

Life opens up a crack; in my family children, and *only* children, are in the wrong. It has always been my fault, especially, and yet here is a grown-up, and a big and important grown-up, siding with the children, of whom I am one, without making a fight about it.

I suddenly see that we had not purposely rusted the troughs, and that Uncle Ed should not have — but I can't go on.

Annette and Veronica go home on Wednesday; I stay till Thursday morning.

After breakfast I go out, at Grandma's request, to empty the teapot in the gully-trap, taking great care, as I have been taught, not to bash the spout on the tap.

Grandpa spots me.

'What are you doing?' he roars. 'Are you trying to block up all the pipes in the street, tipping that stuff down there?'

This time (perhaps emboldened by Aunt Margaret's protective good sense of the day before) I do answer him back. 'At home we always empty the teapot into the gully-trap!'

There is no holding him.

'Don't tell me those lies! Nobody empties their tea leaves into the gully-trap! It's like all those other lies you've been telling about your mother and father! Little liar!'

I don't stay at Grandma's again. I don't remember whose decision it was, but I don't go back till the day after my mother dies.

OPENING THE DOORS

'Go AND open the garage doors for your father,' says Mother, just before tea.

It's one of my jobs. One I like to do. One I can do without much trouble even though the big weatherboard doors are very heavy, and something I can do that pleases both Mother and Daddy.

But today is a wild day. As soon as I get outside the back door the wind throws dust in my eyes, stands my hair on end, blows my dress up round my ears. It picks up Nick's enamel dish and sends it clattering against the wall of the sleep-out. Then it pretends to be gentle and I make a little run and head for the garage, but suddenly with a shriek and a scream it upends the galvanised-iron rubbish-bin and rattles it round the yard, scattering potato peelings and soup bones and empty jam tins everywhere, the lid rattling off in one direction and the bin in the other.

There's another lull. I make it to the garage doors, manage to slide up the bolt on the outside and get inside. I push on one door, harder and harder, and get it a bit open, but the wind is on the other side of the door pushing us back. We battle it out, the wind and I, till the wind suddenly gives in. With a great rush I get the door over onto the grass at the side and wedge a half-brick up against it. Hurrah! The door holds.

The wind starts playing again now, as I walk back to the other door, and comes in little puffs and pants, very friendly, and I think this door will be easy, because the wind is behind me. But suddenly it swirls round the half brick, pushes against it and moves it, and the door crackles and roars and comes after me. It hits me a mighty wallop on the head and throws me into the air.

When I come down again, I am lying somewhere very soft, and above me I hear Mother's voice and Daddy's voice, Daddy's voices, murmuring, murmuring above me as I have heard them many times before.

'Bit of a bump on the head. Just leave her to come to. She'll be all right,' Daddy's voice is saying.

And Mother: 'And what about your father? Is he any better?'

'Died. This morning. About eleven. Ma's pretty upset. Don't know why she should be! She knew it was coming.'

The next voice is Daddy's other voice, which I hear only in my head: *'Time he went, the old bugger! Now we'll see!'*

As I lie listening, my eyes still tightly closed, another voice is stirring inside me, a small voice that I have not heard for a long time. My own voice. I open my eyes.

'Ha!' says Daddy. 'Awake again, are we? You've had a bit of a knock on the head.' And he runs his hand over a sore spot on the back of my head.

'She'll be all right!' he says to Mother. 'Got a lump there as big as an egg. She might be a bit groggy for a while, but she'll be all right.'

They leave me on the bed in the sleep-out while Mother goes to get the tea. I close my eyes again, and their murmurs wash over me from the kitchen, a long way off.

When Mother calls us all for tea, I get up and head for the kitchen, a little unsteady on my feet, but not groggy, no, not at all groggy. At the kitchen door, clear-headed, I stare first at Mother and then at Daddy, and something in the quality of my staring makes everybody stop what they are doing, and fall silent, and stare back. Into that silence I say quite low, but very clear, the first serious words I have spoken to them for years, 'It was you!' I say to my father. 'And you!' to my mother. 'It wasn't me at all that —'

Daddy suddenly rushes at me screaming: 'Quick! Quick! Stop her! She's gone mad! She'll kill someone! She's done it before! She's dangerous! Stop her! Grab her!'

And he flings himself upon me and everyone comes screaming and rushing at me.

Then I do go mad. I kick and I bite and I scream and I claw, but they pin me down, and the ambulance comes again.

This time, when I come home from hospital, I am a

changed girl. I am pleasant and kind and obedient, and for me the best thing is that I can talk again. Another best is that Mother buys me a pink dress, not a sissy pink, like babies wear, but a lovely pink called vieux rose, which means, in French, old rose.

Mother looks at me, when I try it on, as though she is seeing me for the first time.

'It really suits you!' she says, not at me, or about me, but *to* me. 'And it's such a relief for her to have something she looks decent in, so I won't have to be ashamed to take her out. And that new rayon stuff washes like a rag! You look really nice.'

I wear it till it drops off.

Daddy approves of the new me too.

'She's learned which side her bread is buttered on!' he says. 'We won't have any more trouble with her.'

I still stop in the middle of a sentence for no apparent reason, and withdraw into long silences till someone snaps his fingers, or says 'Boo!' or 'Wake up, zombie!' to bring me back to present reality, but my own small voice is mercifully silent.

At school I get told off sometimes for not paying attention, and I develop a technique for looking as though I am listening so that I can give the right answer while another part of me can swim off somewhere else. Some of the teachers are not fooled, and study me intently till I begin to squirm, but they soon give up. I am no trouble, my work is very good, though untidy, and I don't talk in class. The teachers have their own techniques, too, when the class begins

63

to wriggle and get noisy. It's 'Hands on heads!' or 'Hands behind backs!' and we sit in one of these positions for perhaps five minutes till order and discipline are restored. It is all done without violence, generally without even shouting, I think because we acquiesce and are grateful for the few minutes of peace and order; time out, as it were, from the hurly-burly of home and classroom and playground.

In Donkey Dobbs' grade six at the top of the staircase near our room, the story is very different. I often hear his great bellowing voice and the Thwack! Thwack! of his strap on an upturned palm, and I quake in my shoes. Sometimes I even hear him roar: 'Jock Wiltshire! Out here!' And though I am one floor down and Donkey Dobbs doesn't even know of my existence, I shake with fear. Next year I will be in grade six, and I think that if I have to go into Donkey Dobbs' room I will have to run away.

By some miracle I avoid him, and my sixth-grade teacher is remarkable only for having long, strong black hairs on the back of his hands and fair wispy ones on his head. He has go-ahead ideas. Once he sets us to write a story. The writers are to be allowed to read their story out the front of the class. One of the boys is put in charge of a kerosene tin, with orders to bang on it with a drumstick borrowed from the school band as soon as the budding author says 'Um' or 'Er'. I am delighted at the prospect of writing a story and showing off out the front, and I struggle over it for days in secret, but when the great moment comes the only thing that comes out of me is 'um-er-um-er' over and over again, to the accompaniment of a roll of drums suitable for an Anzac Day parade. But even the sea of laughter doesn't cure me. I vow that somehow, sometime, I will tell my story, and people will listen.

This is the year I start falling in love. I fall in love from the other side of the classroom with a new boy called Quentin. He has a strange way of talking, and is the first person I ever saw with a bow-tie. Within a few weeks he has lost both the accent and the bow-tie, and become like the others, and I fall out of love. Next it is Johnny Burke, who, I tell Jock in an incautious moment, as we walk home behind him one day, has beautiful steel grey eyes like Tim McCoy, the hero of the latest Western I have seen at the movies. Jock, the skunk, calls out to Johnny: 'Hey! Burke! She reckons she's your girl!'

Johnny only grins, but that is the last of my confidences to Jock, and the last of Johnny Burke.

The love affair that causes me the most trouble is with C. J. Dennis, who wrote *The Sentimental Bloke*. I see the film at the local picture theatre and immediately become Doreen, the Bloke's beloved. Dennis himself and the Bloke somehow become fused in my mind. I find that Dennis has a poem published every night in *The Herald*, and after studying a few, decide I can easily write one just as good. I wrestle with it, having a lot of trouble with the rhymes, but at last it is finished, and as soon as I get a penny for the stamp I post it off. I hang around the letterbox for a couple of weeks waiting for a reply, but nothing happens, and I forget all about it, as the next crisis strikes.

Lice in my hair! It is a dark disgrace. Muriel, my friend who often walks home with me, starts walking on the other side of the street. It is like having leprosy.

Mother deals with it as well as she deals with most things. First she tries to comb them out with a little black comb with teeth on both sides, and cracks them dead with evident pleasure as they fall onto a newspaper. But my great mop of curly and generally tangled hair is too secure a sanctuary, and the lice win that round. So she sends me off to the barber with a note asking him to cut it all off and run the clippers over it. So here I am sitting in the barber's chair, with a pile of hair all round me on the floor, mercifully not walking away, as Mother had predicted. As I hand over the sixpence to the barber, he says nastily: 'Tell your mother to clean your hair herself, next time.'

'Tell her yourself!' I mutter under my breath, but I am mortified, all the same.

I study my new self in the mirror, and think that even though I have fair skin, my big mouth and my big eyes and my clipped head make me look exactly like a negro, like some slave-girl up for auction in a story I have read. I wonder if anyone would want to buy me? And what happens to the ones no-one wants?

Mother writes me a note for school to say I have had my hair cut off because the doctor said it was taking all my strength, and that I am to keep my beret on in class so I won't get a chill. Nobody is fooled. In class one of the girls wants me to take my beret off, and I won't, and another girl snatches it off and there is a great burst of laughter, and Hairy-Hands is red in the face and furious — with me, of course — for making a disturbance. But it is all rather exciting, in a way.

On the way home Margery, another friend jeers at me: 'Everybody knows why you had your hair cut off. It's because you've got fleas in your hair!'

'Have not!' I jeer back. 'What about you?'

But the triumph of my retort pales into insignificance when I get home.

I collect from the letterbox a pile of letters, mostly with windows, which often means a row, so I drop them quickly on the kitchen table, where Mother and Daddy are sitting drinking tea, and prepare to make myself scarce.

Daddy picks through them, his colour rising till he comes to one that makes him stop.

'What's this?' he says in disbelief. 'It's addressed to you!'

As I begin to realise what it might be, he tears it open, reads it through, and hands over to me my own sheet of spidery writing. 'What's this?'

'It's a poem.' I gulp. 'A poem I wrote. Like C. J. Dennis. You know — the sentimental bloke. I wanted them to put it in the paper.'

He snatches it back, reads it again, throws his head back and laughs, a great guffawing burst of laughter.

'Nobody's going to put garbage like that into the paper!' he says, and screws it up into a ball and throws it on the floor. I crawl away, thankful to escape. I should have known better. I have understood in some dim way that at school I can do the work and be praised for it, but at home to do something well is to invite — well — what I just got.

I should never have tried.

And as I turn to go, I see something begin to prickle at the back of his eyes, something in the set of his lips, in his sudden stillness.

The creature under the rock has moved, and become visible, and he is aware of it.

I must never do anything like that again!

RATS

EXCEPT FOR the rats, this is the best time ever.

Sometimes in the middle of the night we are still awakened by occasional roaring and screaming matches after we have all gone to sleep, and more than once Daddy gets up and throws us all out of the house, barefooted in our nighties and pyjamas, into the icy streets. We walk round for an hour or so till we judge Daddy has gone back to sleep, and it seems safe to creep back inside and into our beds, but apart from this and except for the rats, this is the best time ever.

But the rats! I can hear them when I lie in bed at night, scratching and scrabbling and scampering about, and perhaps dragging something around above my head. I wonder what they can find to eat up there in the ceiling. And I can see them at it with their sharp pointy teeth and glittery eyes, and their long thin tails, as I have seen them in the illustration on the page beside *The Pied Piper of Hamelin* in my school reader.

Eventually the noises in the ceiling get so bad that others hear it too. (So it is not all my imagination!)

'You'll have to do something about those rats in the ceiling, Rex,' says Mother to Daddy at breakfast one morning. 'They kept me awake all night.'

He must have done something while I am at school, though I don't know what, because the noises in the ceiling stop. But I know the rats have not gone.

They are in the yard, so that I am afraid to go out to the gully-trap and empty the teapot after dark.

They gnaw the dahlia bulbs that the gardener has left out to be planted in the spring. They eat the wheat and pollard and the kitchen scraps that we throw through the wire netting into the chook pen. They chew a hole in the hessian bag of pollard stored in the garage, so that a long umbilical cord of it stretches from the garage to a hole under the wall. They eat the food out of the dog's enamel plate when he's not there, and though he rushes round snarling and barking and yelping at his unseen enemy, and digs the holes under the garage walls to make them bigger, he's too old and fat ever to catch any.

Yet except for the rats, this is still the best time ever.

I am in grade five now. Our state school has become very advanced. We are the first school in Victoria to have a swimming pool, built by the mothers' club, and when we get into grade six, we're going to be taught to swim in it. I'm glad I'm not in grade six. I hate cold water and I'm afraid of drowning. As well as the swimming pool, instead of staying in our room all day with one crabby teacher, we're allowed to leave our own classroom and go to special rooms for several periods a week. It is so exciting!

Twice a week, we go to the literature room, where a kind unflappable lady reads wonderful books to us, and lets the best readers read bits of them out the front, and lends them to us so we can finish them at home.

Another day we go to the music room, where Mrs McPhee teaches us to sing. Not the boring old bang-bang stuff like 'Kookaburra Sits in the Old Gum-tree', but *real* songs: 'Danny Boy', 'Loch Lomond', 'Funiculi Funicula' and 'O Sole Mio'.

'I shouldn't be teaching you these songs,' she says to us with great seriousness, 'because the greatest singers in the world have sung them. If you sing them, you'll have to sing them really well!'

For her, we become the greatest singers in the world. I sing those songs even at home, till everyone is sick to death of me and shuts me up, but they are still there, singing in my head, and nothing can take them away from me.

Mrs McPhee teaches me something else I never forget.

As well as singing she teaches us history, and one day I am late for school — well, Jock and I are nearly always late for school. Either we have slept in, or we have had to go to the corner shop for something, or we have put on the clothes we left lying in a heap on the floor last night, and look so weird and unwashed and uncombed that it registers even with Mother, and we have to be told off and smartened up before we go. It all takes time.

When we are late we have to go to the office, where a long-running battle goes on between Jock and Mr Fenton, the headmaster.

Mr Fenton enjoys giving Jock the strap as hard as he can, and Jock enjoys tossing his head and grinning, as if to say: 'Didn't hurt! Didn't hurt!' I always feel that Jock has won the battle, somehow.

This battle goes back to the time when our current huge mongrel dog, called Nick (they were always called Nick), followed us to school, and as Mr Fenwick brought his strap down on Jock's outstretched hand, Nick suddenly appeared out of nowhere, hurled himself at Mr Fenwick's arm and grabbed the strap and Mr Fenwick's arm with it, snarling horribly.

I suppose we must have called him off, or he would never have let go. The next thing I remember is that Jock and I were taking the dog home, Jock doing a kind of war-dance, and stopping every now and then to pat Nick and embrace his big, ugly, delighted head.

The morning inevitably comes when Jock is home sick, and I have to go by myself. As usual I am late, and too scared to go to the office alone, so as no-one seems to be about, I creep up the stairs into Mrs McPhee's room. She makes no comment about me being late, but bids me stand up, just as slimy Mr Fenton comes into the room.

'Ah ha!' he purrs. 'This is the little girl who is so often late. But you weren't late today, were you?'

Everyone in the class knows that I was late, and Mrs McPhee knows, and I feel quite sure he knows, too, so I just nod.

Mrs McPhee enters the arena.

'Emma is just about to read to the class her essay on General Wolfe and the battle of Quebec. It is the best essay for the week, and we are going to put it in our special book, with the other best ones. Perhaps you would like to stay and listen to it?'

What could he say?

She is the first woman I have seen who protected me, who got a man to do what she wanted, and without screaming and without making him look a fool.

There are other people at the school I remember with pleasure, too.

One day a week we go to the art room, where a handsome young man softens the intricacies of drawing ellipses by showing us six cardboard circles, which he has fixed in a long row onto a piece of board.

'Look!' he says to us, like a magician. 'Here we have six circles. All agree? Six circles?' We nod solemnly.

He takes his board with the circles to the far side of the room, and shows us how the ones furthest away have become, not circles now, but ellipses.

So you don't always see what you think you see.

As well as the ellipses, he introduces us to Reeves Greyhound pastels, in rich vibrant colours, and gives us pieces of thick grey and brown and fawn paper to use them on. He lets us draw what we like. I draw a magnificent seaside scene with rocks and a sky and sand and blue water. I feel like a genius again. I take it home and Mother likes it.

'She hasn't done that on her own!' snorts Daddy. 'The teacher's done most of it,' and he screws it up and throws it on the floor. He produces some wax crayons, a torn sheet of paper and a bottle of tomato sauce.

'Draw that!' he orders.

My bottle of sauce doesn't really look like a bottle of sauce. The ellipses aren't right, the writing doesn't go on the label properly, and I even smear sauce on it.

'There!' says Daddy. 'Told you she could never do anything by herself!'

I'll show him! I hate him! I will never take anything of mine home again! And I don't — at least not till I win the gold medal.

We are living now in a much grander house than the last two, which have tenants in them to pay them off. This one is in Malvern. Solid brick. Spanish Mission. A gardener to do the garden. A woman to do the washing and ironing. A new Chevrolet in the garage. Daddy is away a lot in the country, selling blocks of cake that his brother Uncle George makes in his factory. Uncle George never comes to see us at home any more, but he and Daddy buy a racehorse together. Though Daddy studies *The Sporting Globe* and *The Truth* racing section every week, and can tell you the sire and dam of every important horse running, he seems to be keeping the gambling within bounds. The letterbox is often full of envelopes with windows on them, but we never seem to be short of money, except for unimportant things like clothes and school books and doctor's bills, which Daddy doesn't believe in.

The racehorse doesn't win, though it is always just about to.

One night, Daddy comes home from work rather late and smelling of beer. Mother senses it as soon as he comes in the door, before he is close enough for her to sniff it, before he has even planted a kiss wide on the side of her face. I think it is a kind of glow about him that gives him away.

When Mother says: 'Rex! You've had a drink!' as though it was the end of the world, he brushes her off quickly.

'Just a couple with the boys! No more than two! Jimmy Barnes dragged me into the pub — wouldn't take no for an answer! Don't worry about me! I'm fine!'

And in that state, fine is the word for him, as he doles out his manna of fish and chips and spins out the yarn of his day's doings, in which he is always more clever and brave than the rest of them; he has talked more interestingly and driven his truck more skilfully and sold more blocks of Wiltshire's Reliable Cake than any of the other men at the factory. As he talks, soon we are all glowing, too, and laughing and enjoying ourselves in a way that never happens with anyone else.

And I feel such confusion in this pleasure, as though it is wrong to be enjoying myself with him, and a kind of eat-drink-and-be-merry-for tomorrow-we-die feeling, but I can never resist the pleasure of experiencing that glow.

So although there are bad scenes still, sometimes there is joy, and a glimmering of a happiness I am not yet prepared to admit to in case it is taken away from me.

Mother's asthma is not yet bad. She seems not unhappy, and that makes us all feel safe. She cooks us sometimes wonderful food — Danish rabbit, braised in butter and herbs. Pots of rich vegetable soup made from sheep's head. A delicious paste to spread on bread, with ground-up meat cooked in some spicy sauce. Once I even remember her singing as she rolled out flaky pastry for a pie. It is a song, she tells me, Daddy used to sing to me and I used to move my head in tune to when I was in my pram:

> *Dance to your Daddy,*
> *My little babby,*
> *Dance to your Daddy, my little lamb;*
> *You shall have a fishy*
> *In a little dishy,*
> *You shall have a fishy when the boat comes in.*

Sometimes when I am home alone with Mother because I am sick, I sit out in the sunny patch in the fernery while Mother talks to Harry. Harry is our beautiful blond blue-eyed baker. He brings in, every day, a great basket filled with lovely fresh loaves, french loaves, tin loaves, and on special days malt loaves and raisin loaves. He and Mother stand and talk, about the races, about what she has read in *The Age*, about the weather. I am just happy to be there with them. Mother is very pregnant; she pats her big stomach and says to Harry, with a laugh, 'How about that?' I wonder is it Daddy's baby or Harry's. I think it must be a boy she is so pleased about it.

The best time of all is when the others are at school and she talks to me about when she was young, before she was married.

Before she and Daddy got married, she tells me, he used to work in an office. And he took some money from the firm's safe and used it to bet on the gee-gees. And when the horses didn't win, he asked Grandmother for the money to put it back.

'If I don't have it,' he said, 'the boss will send me up and I'll go to gaol.'

'I'll only give it to you if you'll promise never to gamble again,' Grandmother said.

And Daddy said: 'Just give me the money, or else. I'm not promising anything!'

Mother gives a funny sort of laugh as she tells me this, but it is somehow scary, too.

The other story is about herself — the only one I ever remember her telling about herself.

'I used to work for this tailor — a Jew, he was — doing hand-finishing on the suits he made. When my work wasn't up to scratch, he'd swell up and go red in the face and stamp and yell, and throw the work at

me. "Sew me dat clean!" he'd roar. "Sew it clean!"'
Mother can hardly tell the story for laughing, and my
eyes grow bigger and bigger as she talks. This is a new
Mother, and I like her much better.

One sunny Sunday morning I am left alone with
Daddy while Mother goes to Grandma's, where I'm
not usually allowed to go. There is the usual
injunction: 'You stay home and look after your
father.'

She hasn't been long gone when Uncle Ed arrives,
carrying a hose. I am glad to see him. He pats me on
the head and pulls his hand away in pretended horror.

'Oh, Red,' he says, 'you've burnt my hand!'

He and Daddy stand in the sun, drinking beer, and I
can tell by the way Uncle Ed is giggling that something
exciting is going to happen. I wonder what the hose is
for, and what they are waiting for.

Soon two men from the factory drive up in a noisy
old truck and come in and have a couple of beers with
Daddy and Uncle Ed and chat for a bit. Then the real
business of the day begins.

They start digging round the holes under the sides
of the wash-house and the garage. They block up every
hole but two, and tamp the ground down hard around
them. They fix one hose to the tap over the gully-trap
and the other one to one of the taps over the troughs
in the wash-house, and push the nozzles well down
into the two holes.

Daddy goes round telling the men what to do, and when he is satisfied all is in order, he shouts: 'Turn on the hoses, Ed!'

We all stand round watching and waiting for a few seconds. Nothing happens. Soon the water starts gurgling and then gushing out of the holes, and the rats begin to follow. They tumble out, falling all over each other and running in all directions in a frenzy of self-preservation. Stationed on either side of each hole is a man armed with a shovel or a spade, ready to flatten them as they come out. And flatten them they do, with great success at first, until they begin to get in each other's way with the spades and shovels and are soon rushing in disorder round the yard, lunging wildly with their spades. Shouts of triumph as a lunge connects! Shouts of disappointment as one misses!

Uncle Ed trips over a hose and falls down, and rats run over him, and he shrieks and covers his face before he springs up and goes at it even more furiously. The dog strains on his chain, red-eyed, maddened by his inability to get at his enemy, and his barking and yelping add to the uproar. The rats squeal.

It is like a war, or a game of cowboys and Indians. I stand at the open double gates, ready to run, almost a spectator, but infected by the excitement. We are the goodies, and the rats are the baddies. I am on the side of the men; I want those rats gone.

Soon there begin to be fewer of them. Some escape through a hole in the fence into next door, some run along the cement path to the front lawn, a territory as alien to them as it is to me.

At last the war is won. The men, strangely silent now, gather up the corpses and throw them in the rubbish bin, with a brick on the lid for an extra precaution. Daddy offers them another beer, but they have lost the taste for it.

'Better get going,' says one, not meeting Daddy's eyes.

'Yeah! Promised to take the kids to the beach,' mumbles the other.

They collect their shovels, throw them in the back of the truck, and roar off.

Uncle Ed stays long enough to roll a cigarette and stick it behind his ear, gather up his hose, and he is gone too, off to meet his newest girlfriend.

I am alone in the house with Daddy.

As he starts to roll up the hose, a fat half-drowned rat staggers through the mud at the side of the garage. She is so groggy that Daddy has time to run and grab a spade.

I say 'she' because of what happens next.

Daddy takes his spade and, with the sharp edge this time, he makes a short sharp jab and cuts her neatly in half, and the white milk from her teats flows onto the black dirt of the yard. She makes no sound.

Daddy gives me a slow, sly, wolfish grin, and I slide to the ground in a sort of half faint.

With the greatest gentleness he carries me inside and lays me on the bed.

WAGGING

ONCE AGAIN we are wagging it from school. This time Neville comes along too. I like Neville because he doesn't talk much, and because he takes no notice of me at all. I like him in spite of his pale blue eyes and his weak chin and his sandy lashes and his stammery voice. I like him because he is clean and tidy and well-dressed, and his soft blond hair always looks as if it has just been combed. Jock and I are more presentable than we used to be, but our tidiness is a surface thing, while Neville's cleanliness is, as our mother used to say of the dirt on the back of our necks and our ears, ingrained. I am always attracted to such clean, clean people, and always, in a very short time, an unease comes over me, and I know I have no right to be among them.

This is not our first wagging expedition.

Once before when Jock was still at primary school, we'd wagged it with another mate of Jock's, called Jim. Jim was definitely not one of the clean ones. This was his second year in Jock's grade, and he was two years in the two grades before, so he was much older than Jock even — a great big lurching sort of a boy with a slobbery mouth and a snotty nose. An old hand at the wagging business, he'd taken Jock along with him to show him this good place he knew of — a piece of neglected bushland a good way from school at the end of my known world. Through it ran a piece of disused railway track, safe enough at ground level where we went onto it, but the ground below it sloped away so steeply that it soon became terrifying, both for the twenty-foot drop to the creek and the rocks below, and for the great gaps between the rotting sleepers. In some parts we had to crawl on our stomachs, holding onto the rails, which by mid-morning were too hot for comfort. I would never have made it but for the worse fear of being labelled 'cowardy cowardy custard' or of being left behind. Here and there were some little wooden railed platforms built out over the emptiness, and though it was hair-raising to stand up and stagger out onto one of them, it gave me some respite from my unshakable belief that at any moment a train was going to come along and cut off my hands or legs.

After a few trips over and back we went down into the bush below. I picked a bunch of nodding greenhoods and early nancies and some bluebell things, but they all wilted in my hot hand almost immediately, so I threw them away. We sat on the bank of the creek and took off our shoes and socks and dabbled our toes in the brown water and ate our lunches, under attack from mosquitoes and larger and more colourful flies than I was used to at home, some shiny green ones and other big brown ones that bit, and so many of them that we had to keep waving our hands to get the sandwiches into our mouths without eating a few flies, too.

By the time the sun told us it was time to go home we were hot and drowsy and smelly. As I was putting my shoes on, there was a whispered conversation between Jock and Jim, then Jock came over to me and said warily: 'Listen. I don't know the way home, but Jim does. Only he'll only show us if you'll show him your you-know-what.'

I looked at Jim. Jim looked at me.

'I'll give you some watermelon if you do,' he said.

'I don't like watermelon,' I said quickly.

'Well,' he said, 'what *do* you want?'

It was not a question I ever remembered being asked before.

I stared at him for a moment, then I said rapidly: 'I'd like a baby like Thumbelina that I could put in a matchbox in my desk, like the other kids say Jessica in grade six has.'

A change came over Jim. He swelled up, and became much bigger. His voice, which had been wheedling, became loud and boastful as he said: 'If that's what you want, I'll soon give it to you!'

I looked at his bigness, and his wet red lips, and the snot around his nose, and the scabs on his knees showing through the holes in his apple-catchers, and I suddenly jumped up and said: 'It's hard to find your way in the bush, but if we follow the railway line —' and I took off.

Thrown off balance by my sudden shift, the boys tagged along behind.

I had a week in bed after that with a fever and vomiting attack. Mrs Blessington from up the street, whose daughter was in Jock's class, told Mother that Jock had wagged it and he got a hiding, and Jennie ran true to form by saying that it was all my fault and that I should have got a hiding too, instead of getting out of it just because I had played sick.

So why on earth — ?

Well, this time we are on a mission. Jock is going to make himself a truck. Isn't he wonderful, to be able to make a truck?

'You'll have to have a battery,' I say wisely.

He seems surprised, as though that hasn't occurred to him, but he agrees, and it turns out he knows exactly where to find one.

He and Neville take a day off from the technical school they now go to, and here we are, Neville and I, tagging along behind Jock, on a piece of railway land beside the rails clearly marked: TRESPASSERS PROSECUTED. There is a box on legs, not even locked; we lift up the hinged front, and there sure enough are four big batteries. Jock dislocates the wires attaching the batteries to something or other, and we are away, as fast as our legs can carry us — a heavy battery for each of the boys — onto the Caulfield racecourse, also not even locked. We settle behind some bushes and pant for a while, and the boys talk, though not about the truck, about Jonesy, who'd given old Hilly-Billy a mouthful of cheek and got six of the best, and about Jacko, who teaches arithmetic and gave Jock three for arithmetic, even though he'd got one sum right.

'When I got home with my report,' says Jock, 'the old man went mad. I'd added a nought but I told him straight: "If you're going to make all that fuss, you might as well know it was only three!"'

Neville is impressed.

The story is mainly true. Jock had come to me first with the terrible three, wanting some advice. I'd suggested that he put a five in front of the three. He was genuinely shocked.

'I couldn't do that!' he said, 'It would be cheating!'

But the suggestion must have had some merit, because he'd added the nought.

When he presented it to Daddy, there was predictably a mighty bellow of rage.

'Thirty! Thirty per cent for arithmetic! Are you stupid? How could a son of mine be so stupid as to get *thirty* for arithmetic!'

Jock then delivered his speech. There was a moment's silence — as outside the door I trembled for our lives — then Daddy clapped his hands on his knees and roared laughing.

You never can tell, with Daddy.

*   *   *

After we've all recovered from the dangers of the mission, we sit down and eat our sandwiches. Neville's have the crusts cut off and are divided into neat little triangles, which seems just right for Neville. They start digging in the mud on the edge of the racecourse lake for yabbies, and even that doesn't seem to interfere with Neville's incredible cleanliness. They get quite a few, but there is little to do with them but pull their legs off and throw them back in.

I begin to worry whether it is time we went home, and to worry about being found out. And with my vivid imagination, I see two trains colliding in mid-air and lots of heads, arms and legs flying in all directions through the air. And of course, it will be all my fault.

Expecting ructions, I suggest we take the batteries back. Neville has no opinion, but Jock says quite cheerfully: 'Well, I haven't got the sultana box or the pram wheels yet. Might as well!'

I suddenly realise that the truck in my head is quite different from the one in his head.

Back we go. Quite leisurely, in broad daylight, in full view of the man in the room with windows all round it, who turns wheels to make the gates across the road open and close, back we go.

Suddenly we become aware of a man running towards us, shouting and yelling and waving his arms. Jock and Neville drop the batteries and run, but I am smaller, and my legs have become lead, and I am soon caught. The railway detective marches me off to the local police station, where a large fat old red-faced policeman says to me quite kindly: 'What have you been doing?'

I tell him simply and honestly about the truck and our reasons for stealing the batteries and our reasons for returning them.

He makes no comment but says: 'I'll have to take you home. What is your name and where do you live?'

'My name's —' I say and I suddenly stop, with a sense of something happening which has happened before, and I know *I must not arrive with a policeman again.*

'Joyce Smith,' I say quickly, 'and I live at 24 Ross Road.'

He begins walking me home.

I begin to realise that he will not leave me till we get home.

I tell him my real name and address.

He takes me home.

He knocks.

Mother opens the door.

I don't remember what happens after that. Now I am out the back with Jock, already home and already furious. 'What did you want to go and get caught for? Now you've got me into trouble again!'

Soon Jennie storms out. (She's been listening at the front door to Mother and the policeman.) 'You ought to be ashamed of yourself! Bringing disgrace on the family!'

Now it's Mother's turn. But she only says what she always says: 'Just you wait till your father comes home.'

We slink back into our schools, where fortunately we haven't been missed. It is two miserable days before Daddy comes home. Mother shepherds him to the fernery out the back and tells him her version, then goes inside, and I am summoned.

He just stares at me till my eyes drop, then he says, with infinite contempt: 'So. You've turned thief.'

A long pause.

'I've done with you!' he says and he turns and walks away.

He doesn't speak to me, nor does Mother, nor Jennie, nor Jock, for a week. After that week he takes me and Jock aside and tells us we are to be charged at the Children's Court with the theft of the batteries. 'But,' he says, 'I've arranged to see a lawyer. When we go to see him, say nothing, nothing at all. Understand? Just let me do all the talking.'

I am not unwilling. My last attack of talking — my any ever attacks of talking — have brought me nothing but grief.

We go one sunny Sunday morning to a house not very different from our own, and Jock and I sit on two padded chairs at the back of the room while Daddy has his talk with the lawyer-man — just another man like other men as far as I can see; his hair is not grey and curly and he doesn't wear a big black cloak thing, like lawyers at the flickers — he is just a man in a suit with short black hair and a moustache, who reminds me of someone I used to know — I think — a long time ago.

He and Daddy lean over the desk and have a very serious conversation, of which I catch only two fragments: 'first her baby brother' and later 'now this business'.

Daddy comes out smiling, gives us both a hug — the good father — and we are all mates again.

My relief is overwhelming and unconditional.

Mother says darkly when we get home: 'You're not out of the woods yet. Just because you've made it up with your father . . .'

I see it as a threat of some kind, but she can't altogether spoil it.

Of course she is right.

One bitter cold morning we drive to the Children's Court, a big square building with pews in it like a church, and sit in silence for a long time. The magistrate comes in and the lawyer and the policeman. There is much shuffling of papers, then the policeman stands up and recites in a sing-song voice how we stole the batteries, not even mentioning the fact that we were caught because we were taking them back.

At this I come out of my trance and see him as a traitor and glare this message at him, and he becomes human again and says in a kind of warm rush: 'But they're good kids, good kids, both of them, and never been in any trouble before, good kids.'

'Thank you,' says the magistrate, a little surprised. He puts on a very stern face and says: 'Of course, the worst thing is the girl giving a false name and address,' (too clever by half again) and then subsides and mumbles through a long rambling speech that seems to mean that as long as we don't do it again . . .

So we are not to be put away for the rest of our lives and we walk free to the car.

Again, the relief is enormous. That night in bed when I wake up, my mind is sharply clear. I hear my heart beating loud and strong and regular in my ear on the pillow and I know I am alive, then my chest becomes constricted, my stomach knots up and I toss about in a kind of terror.

When this leaves me, I see things that are not there.

I see a man — a man very like the lawyer, with black hair and a black moustache. He is having dinner with another man, in a room with big tables with starched white cloths and shiny knives and forks and vases of flowers. They go into a bedroom and play cards together. The lawyer-man hands over some money to the other man who rolls it in with a roll of notes he has taken from his pocket.

'Big enough to choke a horse!' says the lawyer-man, and they both laugh. They take off their trousers and get into the bed together, and under the quilt they roll and gasp and grunt together.

'Got to go and pay my bill,' says lawyer-man, 'got to leave early in the morning.' And he goes out, leaving the other man starting to get dressed.

Now the lawyer-man is sucking through a piece of red pipe that goes into a hole at the back of a car.

'Quick! Into the bottle!' He makes a face and spits.

*   *   *

In the bedroom, the other man is up too, dressed, suddenly in a tearing hurry.

'Got to go. Got to get home. Wife expecting me. Got to rush.' And he is gone.

The headlights of the truck pick out a car stopped on the side of the road. The man from the bedroom waving beside it. Too narrow to pass. High dark mountain above. Dark deep valley below. 'Ran out of petrol. Don't know how. Filled her up this arvo.'

'I've got some in the car,' says the lawyer-man — but as he turns, he hits the other on the side of the head and chuckles to himself. 'Carotid artery. Trick I learned in the army med.' And he chuckles again as he pulls out the roll of notes and transfers it to his own pocket.

Drags the man into the car, pushes, steers it to the edge; it teeters a moment, tilts, and crashes into the valley below.

Back of the truck the bottle — running down, jumping over bushes, round stumps, down to the car — bottle over it — lights newspaper — throws and runs!

Whoom!

Uphill now, panting and gasping, frightened now, struggling.

Into the truck. 'Jesus! Jesus! The battery! Left the fuckin' lights on! Not a spark! Try the starting handle! No!'

Sobbing now. 'Never get out of here! I'm done for.'

Gets out. Running alongside the cabin, he turns the steering wheel and starts pushing. The truck starts sluggishly to move towards the edge, he jumps in and steers. The truck moves slowly down the road.

There have been other things I have seen, like Grandmother and the baby in the well, that I have not told before. But even before that there were things I'd seen, things I had once told, about a man with a moustache, a man dressed like a soldier, with a rising sun brooch in his collar, but I will not remember and what I told then I will never tell again.

This time I will not tell what I have seen. There is no-one I can tell such things to.

I am older now, and this time I know that whatever it is I have seen, it is not a dream, it is not a nightmare. I know that I have been wide awake. It is my imagination, Mother would say. But it is very real.

It is as though I have been blind and am beginning to see again. I know it is very dangerous to see. I do not understand what I am seeing and I see no connection with my daily life. But I am glad to be seeing again, after so long, and it changes something for me.

HARRY GOES WEST

I AM suddenly instantly awake.

What woke me? Some noise in the kitchen? In the bathroom? In the middle of the night?

I wonder what the time is. How long is it since I went to sleep to the pleasant reassuring drone of Mother washing up, Daddy talking to our lovely baker, Harry, who's been boarding with us lately?

I slide out of bed quietly so as not to wake the two little ones sleeping in my room, and in my nightie with bare feet I go out towards the three oblongs of light in the hall.

I meet Daddy.

'Go back to bed,' he says softly.

'I need to go —'

'Go — back — to — bed,' with quiet insistence. 'Don't look back.'

I turn and go back to bed. This time I won't go in. Not again. Not ever again.

I am suddenly very cold. I crawl in beside the baby, my little brother Brian. Brian is one year old. When he was born, our Protestant grandmother would not speak to us for weeks, because she said Brian was a Catholic name. But I love him dearly. He is a replacement for some baby I loved — or imagined? — a long time ago. I snuggle up against him.

When I am warm, I go back to sleep. I dream. In my dream I see a man wearing Mother's old oil-cloth apron. There is some mess on it, dripping onto the floor.

The dream changes.

I see further, right into the kitchen, where the man stands at the kitchen table, which is now a chopping block. His apron is now a butcher's apron, with blue and white stripes. Sagging round his waist is a belt, with a sheath of knives attached to it. He is cutting up meat, piles of meat, with the carving knife, which he sharpens from time to time on a steel. When all the pile is cut up, he stacks it on shiny white butcher's trays. Then he goes into the big freezing chamber, where some sides of beef hang, and gets out some more.

He takes the trays to the wash-house and methodically tips the meat into buckets and basins — the big galvanised garden bucket, the white enamel bucket used for napkins, the big tin washing-up dish from the kitchen.

So much meat!

And then there are the bones — chopped-up bones. They go into the big dirty bag the briquettes come in.

There is an ambulance parked in the drive, and in my dream I see him put the buckets and basins in it.

I can smell his sweat.

In the bathroom, Mother is washing the bath, the floor. Her movements are jerky, like those of the baby's wooden toy man who dances when you pull his string.

My mother has no face, only a grey smudge where her face should be.

I push the dream away.

I stir uneasily in my sleep, and lift my head and look around the room. All is quiet. All is dark.

'A dream,' I say to myself. 'I won't remember it in the morning. Just a dream. A bad dream.' And I push it all away.

I wake to the noise of the family stirring next morning. I hear Jock grab his cornflakes and leave for his technical school. I get up, splash some water on my face, and go out to the kitchen. As I eat my cornflakes, my father comes in, targeting me with his eyes.

'What are you looking so surly about?' he asks.

'I had a bad dream,' I say, avoiding his eyes, and make my escape to school.

School has been good this year. When I started at the central school last year, for the first time no other member of the family accompanied me. Jennie has gone to work, and Jock is at the technical school.

For the first time I begin to have friends, which at primary school had been difficult. I used to have to walk to school with Jock, home and back at lunchtime and after school. He was allowed out to play after school, I never.

'I need you at home to help me,' says Mother.

At first the freedom of being alone in a new school goes to my head. I play. I talk and laugh in class and out of it. I get picked for the rounders team. I get everything right without even trying. I grow light-hearted and sing. I learn all the words of all the songs in the hit parade.

It couldn't last, of course. At the end of the year my form teacher, Mr Jenkinson, gives me a bad report.

'Work good. Conduct poor,' the report says, under the string of As.

Daddy hits the roof.

'She's been down the shelter-shed with the boys!' he roars to Mother, and to me: 'What have you been up to?'

All I could think of was that I had talked too much, and that would be the worst thing to say. And it was only in Mr Jenkinson's class because he can't keep order and is always sick. With young Mr Fry, who the other kids say has a twin brother, and who is as handsome as a prince, and with Miss Bennet, who is strict but fair, I am a model pupil. If one of them, or Mr Burke who teaches maths and likes me because I get everything right, had written the report, I am sure they would not have written anything so cruel and dangerous.

So instead of answering, I seize up, which makes Daddy madder than ever. I wonder if it is really the string of As that upset him. Once more I have been too clever by half and know too much for my own good.

After the night of the bad dream, it is pleasant to eat my lunch in the schoolyard on some broken-down desks that are stored under the pine trees, not playing, just sitting in the sun talking to my second-best friend, brown-skinned, almond-eyed Sybil, from over the sea somewhere.

My special friend at central school is Norma, who doesn't wear school uniform but a series of beautiful dresses, a different one for each day, and always with socks and a ribbon to match. She seems to come from a different world. Just to see what that world is like, I go with Norma to her place after school one day, in my frayed and unpressed tunic and the shoes with the cardboard inside the soles for the holes.

'Won't your mother be wondering where you are?' asks Norma's mother, after a brief inspection.

'She's going to say she was kept in,' says Norma.

'She shouldn't tell her mother lies!' says Norma's mother sharply.

It seems mothers are the same in all worlds.

Once Norma was to come to visit me at home. I can't imagine how that was allowed to happen. It never happened before.

'I've got enough to do without other people's kids!'

'I'm too sick to have visitors!'

'You've got your brothers and sisters to play with. What more do you want?'

The reasons went on and on.

But this day, for some reason, there is big excitement. I am spruced up in a dress that Jennie has grown out of, and Jennie and I walk to the tram terminus to meet Norma. We arrive so late that Norma has gone home. I burst into such a storm of weeping that Mother is frightened; there's ringing up and Norma finally arrives, but the strain is too much for me and I don't invite anyone else for years.

On the day of the dream, Norma isn't at school, so it is just me and Sybil. We have come out of a science lesson in which we learnt about the solar system, planets, stars, infinity — exciting, mind-boggling stuff, presenting vistas of worlds outside earth, where you never know what might happen.

'I wonder,' I say to Sybil, 'if there is a god for all the other worlds, or if our god is the only one?'

Sybil answers with absolute certainty: 'The Bible says our God is the only God, world without end.'

As Sybil finishes speaking, I suddenly jump up.

'I have to go home for something.'

I run the three blocks home. At the gate I meet Mother with a basket under her arm, going shopping. She has her face on now, but it is still grey.

'Mother,' I say urgently, 'Where's Harry?'

My mother answers me dully, without meeting my eyes: 'He had to go to Western Australia. For the funeral. His father died.'

'I've forgotten my French book,' I say slowly. 'I have to go in and get it.'

'The door's open,' she says, as she walks away.

I go to the kitchen — clean. To the bathroom — clean. To the wash-house. The door is locked. I climb up on the tap over the gully-trap and rub a space so I can see through the grimy window. The troughs are clean and empty; the buckets stacked in one of them, the basins in the other.

The wash-house has a new, wet cement floor.

I jump off the tap and run back to school so fast that my breath hurts me as it goes in and out. On the way I see the parts of the dream that I had pushed away — the man's truck turning into the side entrance of the zoo where Daddy made his cake deliveries once a month.

When I get back to school, the playground is almost bare. I see the pine trees waving in the wind, the broken-down desks. I hear the drums beating for the children to march into school.

As I stand last in line and begin to march in, I begin to cry, not hysterically, but unrestrainedly, with no words, but with such a depth of grief and anguish that the other kids in the line turn and stare at me, appalled.

In the classroom, the teacher — one I like well enough — keeps asking, first me, then as I obviously can't be reached, the other children: 'What happened? What made her cry? Was there a fight? Did someone hit her?'

Nobody answers. Nobody seems to know. They begin to murmur among themselves.

Finally one of the boys speaks out: 'She just suddenly started crying. Nothing happened. Nothing.

Nobody touched her. She just suddenly started, for no reason at all, when she got into line. She's queer!'

The word 'queer' reaches into my mind. And as it does, my crying begins to subside and some words of my own begin to form in my mind.

'*Nobody will ever believe this has happened. I must stop crying. It was a dream. A bad dream.*'

'All get on with your work now!' says the teacher, with a sharp edge to her voice.

I pick up my pen, and start copying from the blackboard in my very best hand-writing: 'The South Island of New Zealand stretches from latitude . . .'

DUCKS

Now that Harry has gone west, everything changes for me. I have made a secret resolution — not the first, but the others have mainly been *nevers* — I will never answer back or talk to strangers, or listen to what doesn't concern me, or tell lies, or tell on anyone, or trust anyone again, on and on, etc. etc.; this one is different. It is not a *never*. This time it is an *I will: I will do what I can for the rest of the family, but I will look after myself, too.*

I don't see this as a good resolution (as all the others were meant to be) and though of course I don't announce it, it probably shows in a hundred ways.

I win a race at a Chevrolet picnic and as I cross the finishing line some man yells at me from the sidelines: 'Ginger for pluck!' I get a bag of lollies for my win. It is my first triumph. Daddy, as usual, snorts, and instructs Mother: 'Don't let her win anything else! She's too big for her boots already!'

Later I will remember the deep thrill of absolute triumph, like nothing I had ever experienced before, that accompanied that win. My first win! And I secretly think: '*I won it and nothing can take that away from me! And I'll win if I want to!*'

My looking-after-myself policy brings a barrage of 'Me, me, me! That's all you ever think of!' and 'Self first, self second, self all the time!' from Mother, and 'Think you're smart, don't you?' from Jock, repeated like a ten-times table. I hear it all, I accept it as true, but I go right on doing it.

I have formed the intention of being like Mrs McPhee from primary school, who somehow escaped the taboo of being married while still teaching school, and who not only saved me from the headmaster when I came late, and allowed me to read my essay out the front, but even praised me. I credit her with an almost protective wisdom, in that she both taught me to sing, so that I could talk at school, and gave me the courage to sing at home. At the central school I have begun soaking up knowledge, as Jock has begun soaking up everything about cars or radios, and as Mother has begun soaking up Abbotsford Invalid Stout (for her health). I accept the fact that most boys and some girls hate girls who get top marks, and I am not deterred.

I am learning other things too, besides schoolwork. Even as I am concentrating on my work, I am watching and listening.

I watch Miss O'Neill, with her hair in long plaits around her ears, and I wonder if she can still hear properly. I wonder why we all do everything she wants in art and history, without her ever having to roar like Mr Burke or get snarky like Miss Phillips.

I watch handsome blue-eyed Mr Leonard, the science teacher, who gave us the solar system and who does marvellous tricks, like the one with the bike pump sucking the air out of a kerosene tin, so that it collapses noisily and spectacularly to prove that the air outside the tin is exerting pressure. Is he married? Nobody knows, but we all agree that he is probably too old not to be.

I watch Miss Phillips, 'Gertie', the Shakespeare lady, who never actually teaches us anything, but writes instructions on the blackboard: 'Write an essay on Autumn in Melbourne' or 'A Day at the Beach', or 'Write a summary of The Merchant of Venice, Act three, Scene two', which requires all my concentration, given the Shakespearean language, even though it is explained in the notes.

Gertie never corrects anything we do, so it is a choice between sly games of noughts and crosses and squares, or drawing faces, or Shakespeare. I try the games for a while, but they soon get boring, and I am hopeless at faces, and Shakespeare turns out to be a good read — a much better read than the paperback westerns I get at home. I am full of admiration for Portia for picking the right casket, thus ensuring the happy ending I crave. I think she's a bit mean not to let Shylock go at the end, seeing that he'd lost both his ducats and his daughter, and Antonio is safe and rich again (I really would like everyone to be happy). And I wish I could have managed my day in court as well as she managed hers.

Even as I concentrate on all this, I am watching and listening too. As soon as we are settled in with our essays or our summaries or our noughts and crosses, in comes Mr Miles, the teacher of grade six. (What has he done with grade six, and isn't he frightened of the headmaster, surly Mr Trumble?)

Evidently not, for he and Miss Phillips talk and smile and she bats her eyes and they look into each other's eyes, and if Miss Phillips has to rebuke a fidgeter or a giggler, she does it pleasantly and firmly without being put off her stroke for more than a second. It is as good as bits of the Saturday arvo movies. The other kids add spice by telling me with shocked delight: 'He has a lovely wife and children at home.'

How do they know such things? The same way I now know them, I suppose.

The last two periods on Friday afternoon always used to be the worst time at school, but in central school the folding doors separating the two biggest classrooms are opened and we all mill in, squeezing three or four to a desk.

Gertie is now transformed. She plays a little hurdy-gurdy organ, two of the men write the words on the blackboard and eject the troublemakers, and we sing. We learn dozens of songs: the best of Gilbert and Sullivan, school songs, hymns, folk songs and even a few popular songs, all mixed up together, and at such a rattling pace that nobody has time to draw breath or play up, and I can't believe it when the bell rings and it is time to go home.

And before I can believe it, it is time to leave central school, too.

With a competitiveness and doggedness till then uncharacteristic of me, I have managed to be top of the class again and beat my only serious rival, Pat Alton, a false friend who has somehow got wind of the battery-stealing episode and drops little smiling hints among my friends.

'I don't know what you're talking about,' I lie. But I shrink, remembering at some deep level Mother's pronouncement that God will strike me dead if I tell lies.

When I am top of the class this time I am also, somehow, dux of the school.

One morning as I stand in line at assembly, not listening to Mr Trumble droning on, the kids around me start poking and prodding me: 'Emma! Emma! It's you! It's you!', and Gertie moves fast: 'Quick, Emma! Wake up! Out the front, Emma! Go out to Mr Trumble!' She propels me in the right direction, and I go.

What have I done? I head out the front, past all the long rows with their teachers beside them, up the long ramp to the platform at the top, where the headmaster stands, very important, with a little box in his hand.

But Mr Trumble, who in my two years at the central school has never been known to crack a smile, is beaming at me like an old pal. He moves the box towards me, a box with the lid off and a gold medal nestling on a piece of cotton wool inside it. I think for a minute he is going to give it to me, but he doesn't.

'I present you,' he says in loud solemn tones, not to me, but for the whole school to hear, 'with this medal for your good work in being dux of the school. Put your hands together, school, for this year's dux!' He claps, and the whole school dutifully claps, probably just as much in the dark as to what a dux is as I am. He gives me the medal.

I say nothing, which is what is expected.

Back in the grade all the kids press round, wanting a look. The one who clears up the mystery is Pat Alton, who'd probably wanted to be dux herself.

'It only means you were top of the last class in the school. That's all!'

I go home at lunchtime with my medal, which I refuse to be parted from, and with a sealed envelope addressed to Mother containing a letter asking her to come back that afternoon for a meeting with Mr Burke, the maths teacher, the roarer, the head of the central school. Her consternation is almost as great as mine, but her curiosity wins, and we go together for our mutual protection.

We need not have worried. Mr Burke, who's always been very kind to me when he's not roaring, asks for a look at the medal, which I'm still clutching, and then speaks to Mother.

'How nice for you to have your daughter doing so well!' he says to her. 'You must be very proud of her!'

We are both dumbfounded.

'I think she's brilliant!' he says. 'Often she doesn't

seem to be listening to a word I say, but she's taking it all in, and she remembers it all!'

Panic! This is not the kind of information I want Mother to be hearing! But Mr Burke goes on and on.

'I have arranged for her to go to the new Melbourne Girls' High School, the best school in Victoria! On my recommendation' — he swells a little — 'they have agreed to by-pass the usual entrance examination and admit her. I am sure she will do very well.'

He has it all arranged, and he is so used to giving the orders and being obeyed that neither he nor Mother can contemplate any argument.

We arrive home that afternoon. At teatime Mother breaks the news, the medal is exhibited, passed from hand to hand, turned over, the inscription read silently by everyone a few times, and though at first there is little response except mystification, I sense a sort of subterranean rumble, as though there might be volcanoes or earthquakes or tidal waves about.

Jennie is the first to erupt. She has always been considered much smarter than I am and she explodes now in fury. Why wasn't she given this opportunity? That stupid headmaster at the school she went to had advised them to send her to business college, and now this seems much better.

But no-one is listening.

Daddy has said nothing at all, but now his rage surfaces.

'I've got no money for school fees!' he roars. 'Where am I going to get nine pounds a year?'

'*The same place you got the money for Jennie's business college*!' I mutter under my breath, but fortunately he is too enraged to notice.

Mother says nothing, perhaps torn between her oft-stated conviction that education is for boys (girls only get married and it's all wasted) and a feeling that against all the odds, I might be turning out to be something of a credit to her. I am, after all, *her* daughter.

There is some triumph in it too, for me, though I take care not to let it show. My medal is inscribed to EMMA WILTSHIRE, DUX OF THE SCHOOL. It is real. It has happened. It is mine. Even Jock saying: 'She couldn't do that by herself! She must have copied!', can't take it away from me.

I lie low. My opinion is not asked for. I am a straw in the wind.

Into the maelstrom swoops Grandmother Wiltshire, the melon-thrower, another one who is used to giving orders.

She whisks me off to Sandringham without explanation. She takes me out at night to meetings of the Rechabite Lodge, where there are a lot of young people, all very friendly; they teach me to play carpet bowls, and I sign a paper which makes me a member of the lodge, and I swear never to touch alcohol as long as I live. Next I become a member of the Loyal Orange Lodge, where they are just as friendly, but I resist signing anything because I think I am supposed to hate Catholics for the rest of my life. One Saturday morning the purpose of all this becomes clear when Grandmother takes me to a cold bare hall, where I sit for scholarship examinations donated by the two lodges. One of them, worth twelve pounds a year, I win. It is enough to pay the school fees.

It is with some triumph that Grandmother tells Daddy about the trips to the lodge meetings, and how much I had enjoyed them and how I'd won the scholarship.

Daddy is strangely disturbed, as he was once before when someone had asked me to join the girl guides.

'Don't let her get in with any of those cliques!' he said. 'She'll start getting friendly with them and talk her head off, and then we're done for.'

Now he mutters about people sticking their noses in between a man and his children, but he is wary of going against Grandmother's accomplished fact and he warns me against the course I am following.

'You won't last five minutes in a snobby school like that!' he fumes. 'They'll eat you alive! I went to Wesley College for a year when I was a bit younger than you, and they all hated me because I came from Brunswick!'

And he warns me against the stultifying effects of too much education.

'Look at your cousin Kenneth!' he fumes. 'Degrees from university, and in the diplomatic service, and yet he can't add up two rows of figures without making a mistake! And look at your cousin Alice! What good did it do her to be good at her books and become a lawyer? She's an old maid!'

An awful fate indeed!

I remember Kenneth and Alice, both very solemn and grown-up and disapproving, but I remember also their younger brother Laurie, and he too was good at his books and went to university, studying something called Ag. Science.

He was red-haired and freckled, and when I met him he was laughing with excitement as he told Grandmother how he'd just won the prize for picking the best bull at the Royal Melbourne show. Being good at his books didn't seem to have blighted *his* life.

Perhaps even girls . . . ?

At last, after warnings that he'd take me away if I didn't do well, he coughs up the money for train fares and school uniform, and I walk the long walk along St Kilda Road to Melbourne Girls' High School, situated at that time in the less grand parts of Government House. The governor and his retinue have been transferred (to avoid the cost of its upkeep during the depression) to the Windsor Hotel.

In these surroundings I feel as strange as Mickey Rooney in Buckingham Palace and for a long time concentrate most of my efforts on not being noticed. Some of the teachers really know how to teach, and as I gradually relax and lose my fear of being eaten alive, the work becomes easy and I begin to enjoy myself. I love algebra, with its problems and solutions, and the beautiful logic of geometry. History is changed. Instead of lists of kings and queens and battles in England, or Australian explorers who went on dreary journeys into the centre of Australia and died of thirst without accomplishing anything that I could see, history begins to be about people.

At first it is about Christendom in the Middle Ages, where everybody had his place and there was a place for everyone. There are pictures of beautifully illustrated books in writing I cannot understand, and a little book called *Lord's Men of Littlebourne* which we all had. In it there is a kind Lord and his Lady and a lot of serfs all working the land dutifully and happily. It beats primary school history — or life, for that matter — hollow. I suspect I would have been a serf if I had been born in those days.

My inevitable fall from virtue occurs in sewing class. Every Monday afternoon, we do nothing but sew. It is terribly boring. I knit myself a beanie and scarf, which turn out well, and in which I fancy myself no end until Daddy tells Mother that I am not to wear it again. 'She looks like a tart in that get-up!' he says.

The only other garment I complete is a school blouse with raggy buttonholes. Fortunately I never have to do them up, because my expanding breasts mean that I have grown out of it long before it is finished. I notice that the teacher never calls the roll, so every Monday I play the wag again. (How did I dare?) I just put on my hat and walk out of the place. I can only assume that I had become as invisible as I tried to be, or that given my good work and general virtue, everybody thought someone else had given me permission. I go into town and spend my week's pocket money on a film at the Regent or the Athenaeum and escape into some of the best films I have ever seen.

As a small child I used to go with Jennie and Jock to the local movie-house where on Saturday arvos we could escape for threepence into wonderful black and white and, at first, silent films. There were Judy Garland and Mickey Rooney in *Our Gang* serials, lots of cowboy and Indian films, love films, and frightful comedies. The audience of adult-free children would stamp and roar to show our approval or disapproval, and a lady played the piano loudly in the intervals. Once after *The Student Prince* we rushed home for an explanation because contrary to established procedure the man didn't get the girl, and we thought they must have finished it before the end. Mother laughed, but didn't explain. Another time, after a film in which one Michael Strogoff, about to be blinded by the baddies, was saved because the tears he shed for his dear old mother prevented the sword from penetrating his eyeballs, I'd come home in such a sodden mess from the tears I'd shed for poor Michael that none of us were allowed to go to the movies for ages. Was I popular! It was probably in this pause that I worked out that the Ginger Meggs cartoons were just drawings, but that the people in the flickers were real people pretending to be an Indian brave or Robin

Hood who had been dead for years, and that when it was over they stopped pretending and they could go home and just be themselves. It looked such fun that I wished I could do it. But it didn't stop me from bawling at movies when alone again.

I think it was the memory of those happy Saturdays that powered me to try the wagging again at high school.

Auntie stops me before I can get caught.

We go to Grandmother's one night, and suddenly in the midst of one of those relations-type conversations about nothing much, Auntie Doll says, poker-faced, to Daddy: 'Rex, have you seen that show at the Athenaeum? Robert Donat in *The Ghost Goes West*? You should see it! You'd love it!'

I begin to take notice. She looks me in the eyes and says, smiling: 'I meet some interesting people at the movies!'

Before my shock has time to register on the others, she has whisked me out to the kitchen to help her make some tea. Mother has picked up on something, and follows us out closely, but not before Auntie has had time to hiss in my ear: 'Don't worry, Emma! I won't ever give you away.'

I have an ally again! The world changes for me.

DEPRESSION YEARS

IT IS 1934, the year of Melbourne's centenary. It is a hundred years since Batman did his famous trade with the Aborigines — beads for land.

The owner of MacRobertson's Chocolates donates a huge sum of money to build the Swan Street bridge over the Yarra River and the first secular secondary school in Victoria for girls. The governor and his entourage have moved back into Buckingham Palace and after a brief stint in a dilapidated old school in West Melbourne, we move into MacRobertson Girls' High School, a very new, very square, very ugly (compared to Government House) building, inevitably christened by the boys of Melbourne Boys' High 'The Chocolate Factory'. In the four years I spend at high school, we are taught in three different sites, but throughout these upheavals I am sustained by a sense of security borne of the recognition that the staff remains the same, they have something to offer which I want and need, and that because I am prepared to work, I have something to offer which they appreciate.

Life at home during those four years is only moderately chaotic by Wiltshire standards.

After the bankruptcy the cake factory is closed, there is some dispute about Daddy's accounts and it is Uncle George's turn to disappear from even the outskirts of our lives — this time for ever. The tenants move out of our two houses, and we lose all three, along with the Chevrolet, the gardener, the washing and ironing lady, and Mother's engagement ring.

Mother's asthma has become steadily worse since Harry went west. She attends the asthma clinic at the Alfred Hospital, where they are very kind to her and provide her with a syringe and a bottle of Parke-Davis adrenalin. They teach her to inject herself when an attack comes on, and at first it works miracles, but the attacks become more and more frequent, so that sometimes she is injecting herself seven or eight times a day. Later she often neglects to clean the needles as she has been taught, so her arms in her sleeveless dresses are covered with a mess of half-healed scabs which she wears as a badge of her sufferings.

I stir in my sleep at night and hear her on her knees in bed, coughing and wheezing and gasping for breath, and though I will myself back to sleep, the frightfulness of hearing her fight for every breath does not leave me.

She has begun to believe that a change of air helps her breathing, so we move at first to Caulfield to be near our schools then, as every street in every suburb has several empty houses as a result of the depression, we move to Brighton, to three houses in one street in Murrumbeena (though the air at one end of the street could hardly have been much different from the air at the other end), then to two houses at Camberwell, to a beautiful two-storey house in Ivanhoe near the river, to Northcote, to Brunswick, to Malvern, to Chadstone, to Caulfield, and back to Malvern. The caretaking aunt's husband made cracks about us not paying the rent, but I think the rents must have been paid, or all those estate agents would not have been so ready to find us another one. In all these moves nobody complains; everybody helps with the packing and unpacking; Daddy tears up linoleum or carpets and tacks or lays them down again without protest.

Some of these moves are to dwellings behind shops, where Daddy now sells console wireless sets, some of them powered by big square batteries. These bring the A.B.C. news and the music and the serial *Blue Hills* to areas like Springvale and Templestowe where the electricity has not yet reached, and they sell like hot cakes. There is always some businessman who is impressed by the fluency of my father's tongue and his often brilliant ideas and is willing to finance him in his ventures, and always, sooner or later, they all fold. It is the financial climate, or the banks, 'which always put the squeeze on me just when I was getting it together'.

We are never hungry, but the pile of bills on the mantelpiece sometimes gets bigger and bigger till Daddy has a big win on the races or gets paid for some wirelesses he has sold; then he comes home with the car loaded with meat and fish and fruit and vegetables and groceries from the Victoria market, and we all breathe again.

There are various rows, but since one time — and I was very small — when Mother goaded him over something and he lunged at her and I slid shaking with terror between them, he has not hit anyone for years. He had backed off then, but Mother tried to stir the pot by saying to me: 'What kind of a man hits a woman?' I was so relieved the moment had passed, and so angry with her for trying to prolong it, that I huffed off. But even so long afterwards, the rows revive in me an old fear of going away and leaving her, as though if I were not there to step between them, he just might kill her.

At last he gets a little roof built beside the fernery and attaches to it a punching ball that he pounds for half an hour before and after work. Jock attacks it too, and I would like to try but it is too high, and I am afraid I would not get out of the way quickly enough and it would hit me back.

Jock is now old enough to borrow the car when Daddy is not around, and the inevitable happens when our huge unreliable old second-hand Studebaker breaks down on the far side of Oakleigh and Jock can't get it back. I come home from school twice to hear he has left home never to return. Once he sleeps in the park overnight. Once he stays at Grandmother's for a few days, but he comes home both times and there are grand reconciliations and all is forgiven. It is never quite clear to me who is forgiving who.

Even Jock and I — regarded by the others as 'deaf mates' (meaning that neither of us would take someone else's part against the other) — are not immune. Once, over some real or imagined slight, I catch him off guard and throw him out of the bedroom where I now sleep alone, and he lies on the floor in the hallway amazed, but only his dignity is hurt. Mother and Daddy and Jennie are delighted that the alliance seems to be broken and come in to laugh at him. And then I am enraged with them. I glare at them: 'This is a private fight! The last thing I want is for you lot to be lording it over him!'

Nobody is pleased with me.

The worst dramas are with Jennie, and they are the worst because the row on the surface is not the *real* row, and other things too bad to be even thought of are going on underneath.

While she is still working at the factory, Jennie has opened some letter addressed to Daddy, assuming it was some bill to be paid. Instead it is from a woman from a country town where Daddy sells cake. I never hear what is in the letter, but Jennie is accused of poking her nose into things she doesn't understand, being a bad influence on the younger children (which means she has criticised Daddy), and told to get another job.

'It's always a mistake to have relations working for you!' says Daddy.

Jennie gets a job, not as an office worker, but as a live-in lady's maid to a rich woman in Toorak. She leaves home.

Daddy's rage is monumental.

'Domestic service! With your education!' he roars. 'Haven't you got any self-respect? And how do you expect your mother to manage without you?'

Jennie is not one to withdraw into silence. She is full of some deep elemental pain as well as rage, and she storms back at him with a passion he can't answer: '*My education!* Twelve months at a business college! You call that an education? At least at this job I get the same wages as I did at the factory and I don't have to give nearly all of it back to you in board!'

We are all forbidden to have anything to do with her.

But even Daddy's rage is not just rage. There is fear in it too and consternation, so that though he bars her from the house, he is enormously relieved when she starts slipping back on her Saturday-afternoon-till-Sunday-night off.

It is not the same, though.

On Saturday afternoons she takes to helping out a cousin who has a cake shop, and Susan is another bad influence. Daddy says Susan is a mischief-making bitch. Jennie tells me that Susan thinks Daddy is a bad man. I don't know what to say to all this, but it frightens me to hear her say so, in case Daddy hears her. Mother's influence is strong too, those half-remembered warnings: 'Nobody will like you if you say anything about your father!' and 'Aren't you ashamed talking about your father like that? After all he's done for you!'

Susan teaches Jennie to wear make-up and sends her to a hairdresser and shows her how to wear a beret on the side of her head instead of plonked on top in down-for-the-show style.

'What's that all over your face?' says Daddy, the first time he sees her wearing make-up. 'You look like a tart!' and he wipes it off. But where I might give in, Jennie persists. She even starts to wear lipstick and paint her nails pink. She and Mother begin to have rows, and for a while I am the favourite. Mother couldn't manage without me. I make her cups of tea with boiling milk instead of water to help her keep her strength up, but I know I am a terrible disappointment to her.

'Why can't you be more like other girls?' she groans, as I memorise French verbs or mutter the soliloquies from *Hamlet* as I do the washing-up.

And I know that it is true. I am *not* like other girls. I see Jennie who begins to have a series of boyfriends of all shapes and sizes and kinds. Another aunt gives her wonderful clothes that she has been given by the people she does caretaking for, and Jennie comes home one Saturday night and gets dressed up in a beautiful scarlet georgette dress with a dipped hemline and with her new Eton crop showing off her small perfect ears and accentuating her high cheekbones. I think she looks like a film star. The boyfriend waits while she gets ready, and I hang around and giggle at his lightest word until he is quickly whipped away by Daddy, who gives him a beer and charms him, and when she comes out, it seems as though the boyfriend hardly notices that she looks like a film star.

And I am not sure whether the dressing up is for the boyfriends or directed in some subtle way at Daddy, who seems to be getting some obscure pleasure out of her visits. The boyfriends do not last. She gets into the double bed she shares with me one Saturday night at 1 a.m. after being out with one of them, and tells me that the latest one has gone.

'Nobody will ever want to marry me,' she sobs. 'And it is all God's fault! I hate him! I hate him!'

I am amazed as well as upset. I don't think I believe in God either as saviour or spoiler, though I once saw him as a sort of ally of my mother's who would strike you dead if you told lies or answered Mother back. I don't know what to say to Jennie; she has always seemed to me to be the one who knows everything, and it is a shock to find it is not so.

Soon she leaves her job as a maid and works as a travelling saleslady, selling undies to factory girls. She is desperately hard up, so much so that I secretly meet her every Monday and take her a cut lunch which I have sneaked from home. She now lives in a flat in St Kilda with a Catholic lady who is separated from her husband and having an affair with a man who comes and stays three nights a week. She can't marry him because she is a Catholic and Catholics can't divorce, but she goes to confession every week, so that makes it all right.

It seems a convenient arrangement, I suppose, except that I can't think of anyone I would want to confess my guilty secrets to, as well as feeling that, apart from answering back and sulking and being dux of the school and being too big for my boots and not being grateful for-all-I've-done-for-you and not going out to work as the others did, my really important sins are the ones I've succeeded in forgetting and am determined to go on forgetting. And if I ever did tell someone, it would have to be not a priest, but someone who was married, or he would never understand my secret wish to get married and have a baby myself one day. Soon Jennie herself is having an affair with a man who is married, though he and his wife have long since parted. Jennie hasn't told anyone but me that he is married and I am sworn to secrecy — one more uncomfortable, perhaps dangerous, secret for me to keep. He seems quite nice and soon he is more often at our place than his own.

Once when he and Jennie and I are larking together in the kitchen and everyone else is out, he chases me round the table and kisses me. I'm upset; I burst into tears. Jennie takes me aside and worries: 'Was there anything nasty about the kiss?'

There wasn't — I feel a fool.

'No! No!' I assure her. 'I don't know why I was upset. Silly of me!' and we make peace.

Later I know that what upset me was being kissed by Jennie's boyfriend. If I'm going to be kissed, I want it to be by my own boyfriend, not by someone else's, and especially not by Jennie's, and while I live at home there is no hope of that.

But he has touched something in me that I am not ready to deal with.

HOW DEAD IS DEAD?

So far I have been able to keep my two worlds quite successfully apart. I don't talk about school at home, and I don't talk about home at school. Nobody seems to notice.

In my last year at high school I realise that I will soon have to leave this last sanctuary, where for several hours a day for four years I have been able to push away the dramas of home and occupy myself with something I do well and enjoy. There are plenty of rules, and I generally obey them. I keep my navy blue pleated tunic (now rather short and tight and beginning to look greenish-mauve in some lights) well-pressed, my blouse clean, my hair washed, and if sometimes I have to stuff the heel of my black stockings under my feet because of the holes, I just hope no-one notices.

I know it is peculiar of me to prefer learning about geology and evolution and maths and history to doing womanly work like scrubbing floors and peeling potatoes, but I do. At school they give me work to do and I do it, generally very well. They are pleased, I am pleased.

Nothing has ever got badly out of control at school the way it does at home.

But since Ken kissed me, something *inside me* has suddenly started getting out of control.

To begin with, I, who have never asked questions, start asking awkward questions that make the other girls groan.

'How can people possibly determine the ages of all those rocks so as to be able to classify them?'

The geology teacher gives a rather long and involved reply, but I see that it is possible. I ask Miss Burne, the biology teacher: 'How can you be so sure that a hydra is an animal and not a plant? It looks more like a plant to me.'

Surprise! Surprise! She hushes the groans and says: 'Good question! Because plants and animals have different cell structures.'

Winsome, a very religious friend of mine, starts to get distraught during a lesson on evolution, which I have no problems with, and asks: 'How can you say such things? It goes against everything I have been taught!'

Miss Burne defuses the situation at once by saying briskly: 'That is something you must discuss with your spiritual adviser,' and goes on with the lesson. There is no question of her ridiculing Winsome or blaming her or making her feel small; she is like Mrs McPhee from primary school all over again. I am reassured by such decency; I had begun to wonder if I only imagined that such goodness existed.

The maths teacher is not so accessible. My question: 'Can you explain what sine, cos and tan mean?' annoys her.

'Just use them!' she says tersely.

So when the choice has to be made between maths and science and humanities, I opt for humanities because I don't think I understand maths.

(Do two and two really make four, or is it five?)

Miss Price, who teaches the other class French, is an incredibly thin woman with a pinched pink nose and a pale blue complexion, and she dresses each day in either a pale pink dress, a pale blue dress or a pale grey dress. She fills me with a kind of dread.

One day I read on the notice board an instruction to Form D1 to go for period seven to room 101 for French, as the usual teacher is away.

'Lord!' I say to the girls around me. 'I hope that doesn't mean we're going to have Miss Price!' And my shoulder is clutched by a bony hand which propels me to room 101, a small room set apart at the end of the corridor. There she turns me round till I am facing her.

And she lets forth such a tirade that, terrified as I am, I know she is crazy, and I put up a sort of shield, a barrier between us.

'I know I'm not popular!' she hisses at me. 'And I wouldn't want to be popular with little guttersnipes like you!' On and on, till at last: 'I heard that filthy language you were using!' she hisses — and at this I break. I burst into tears and roar back: 'I didn't use any filthy language! All I said was that I hoped we didn't have you for French! And I hope we never do!'

She is halted for a minute, but she comes back with a kind of desperation.

'When you get out of here,' she says, 'that Rosa Parkes and that lot will all be crowding round you: "What did she say? What did she say?", but I am backing out, shaking, and I leave her still talking.

Outside our own room, there they all are at the door, Rosa and Co, asking, 'What did she say? What did she say?' But I just shake my head and I am saved by the bell.

The safe boundaries I have erected between home and school seem to have been breached, as they were when I got the bad report and was dux of the central school. The separation of the two worlds in which I have managed to operate more or less successfully because they have been kept apart is endangered — will I get a bad report over this?

I slink around for a week or two, expecting a summons from the head, and when none comes, I push it all away into that pit at the bottom of my mind where it lodges undisturbed, but not undisturbing, along with all that undealable-with stuff that has been accumulating there for many years.

I meet Miss Price later in the grounds of the university. She is still wearing pale blue but she is now sporting a shiny new wedding ring. (She must be fifty!) And she is all over me. She congratulates me on my results, on my scholarship, on being dux of the school, as though we were old friends.

But I shrink and back off again. This is another of those things that simply can't be happening.

Meanwhile at school I start having trouble with ghosts.

Banquo was bad enough, and Hamlet's father, but in Latin classes we translate parts of *The Aeneid*, and go with Aeneas into the underworld, where all the most important ghosts of the ancient world are neatly compartmentalised, the best spots being reserved for warrior heroes, the worst for those who struck a parent or hated their brothers, which must have made for a fairly overcrowded area if all families were like mine.

The widow Dido is there, not at all merry, but raging still against Aeneas, who had compromised her in the eyes of the Carthaginian nobility then abandoned her at the prompting of the gods so that he could go off and found the Roman Empire. Rather than face life as what my father referred to contemptuously as another man's leavings, she allays the fears of her loving sister Anna by telling her that she has found a way of recovering from Aeneas' treachery. She will build a huge pyre and on it place all the relics which remind her of someone who must never again be mentioned: the bridal bed, the garments and the sword, and by burning them she will free herself from him for ever. She sends Anna away, climbs on top of it, and sets fire to it, falling to her death on Aeneas' sword.

It is a powerful story, told by a great poet. I am devastated, not least by the prospect of Dido spending the rest of eternity raging helplessly in the underworld.

I myself have never quite forgiven Aeneas for absentmindedly losing Creusa, his first wife and a paragon of all the womanly virtues, during the escape from burning Troy, but Creusa doesn't even rate a mention in the underworld. I know that Aeneas is the hero of this great epic and the mythical founder of the mighty Roman empire, so I leave my questions unasked of the kindly spinster who teaches us Latin.

Meeting all these ghosts gives me a feeling that I am loath to put into words but can't quite get rid of, that I myself have known someone, not in a story, and much later than Jesus or Lazarus, who really was pronounced dead and came back to life, and went on talking and walking just like anybody else.

In year eleven we have a fascinating history teacher, the only daughter in a well-known family of medicos. I remember Jennie's scornful words: 'Women can't be doctors!' when I said I wanted to be one, and I wonder if Miss Nixon minds. She is well-educated, well-travelled, witty, sophisticated, intelligent and good-looking; and she teaches us history like a series of stories, so that it almost seems like an extension of the literature course, talking of kings and queens, popes and protestants, warriors and philosophers, with insight and humour, as though she has known them all personally.

With her in mind, I decide on the subjects for my matriculation year: English, French, and Latin, which I know I will do well at, and European history for — what? Pleasure? Relaxation? Both rather dirty words in my family.

So it may be a judgement on me when they change teachers on us, and instead of our spellbinder we get a large ugly woman, Miss Lehman, who, it is whispered (it is too shocking to be said aloud), is a card-carrying communist. Is she? Who knows?

We begin by loathing her, and some girls never stop, but I can see that she is directing my studies in a way that no-one before (or since) has ever done. She starts always by giving a concise account of the topic to be studied — war, revolution, reformation, whatever — and summarises it under headings on the blackboard. She then provides us with several references — book, title, author, page numbers — all obtainable from the school library. As most of the authors give surprisingly different accounts of the same events, she starts the process of clearing my mind of the myth of simple truths, of a world divided into goodies and baddies, and proposes in its place a world of causes and effects.

She overturns also the system I have got along with very comfortably till now, in which the teacher tells, and we sit and listen, and very little is expected of us except silence. She still tells but she wants it all back, digested and regurgitated, and she knows how to get it. She tests us, corrects our efforts rigorously, bullies us, demands far more than we are prepared to give, and is miserly with marks and with praise, but to her I owe the high first I get in the external exams and yet another way of looking at the world.

I begin swimming in some very deep waters indeed. The me that in central school was upset with Portia for not letting Shylock off the hook begins to take rather a beating. In English literature we are studying in depth some great plays and novels, *Macbeth* and *Hamlet*, and *Tess of the D'Urbevilles*, and the people in them are all people I seem to know: Lady Macbeth egging on her husband to murder someone, Ophelia classed as a whore because she is walking alone and harbouring thoughts of love for 'a prince out of her star', Tess and her bastard baby, the mayor of Casterbridge who sells his wife for a penny when he is drunk at the fair. For all these characters, life is difficult, demanding and dangerous.

Our literature teacher is a devout Catholic: her interpretation of these events, sanctioned by the critics, is that each of these characters has a fatal flaw that brings them to their downfall. I wonder how she gets on in the staffroom with the card-carrying communist.

And if the worlds of history and literature are full of mysteries and marvels, real life, as I see it in the lives of my friends at school, seems to be not so different.

One of my friends is Angela — clever, capable, friendly, matter-of-fact and outspoken — who rescues me when my marks in an art exam fall a little below the pass rate. I am to submit my year's folio of work, and if that is up to standard, I will be passed. I submit it first to Angela and two other friends, who take it home and make various improvements and presto! I have passed! Is it cheating? Probably, but it beats failing.

Angela tells me about her father.

'He's as rich as anything, and he won't spend a penny if he can help it. And he's red in the face and has pains in the head, so he probably won't live long enough to enjoy it.'

I am aghast at such frankness.

Angela invites me home to meet her mother and with some apprehension, I accept. I need not have worried.

Angela's mother wins my heart by feeding me the largest plate of food I have ever had put before me in my life — no meat, only vegetables, many of which I don't even know the names of till she tells me.

Better than the food is the sense of being talked to, of being included in the conversation as an equal that makes this night one of the most memorable and tremulous of my life.

For not only is Angela's mother a vegetarian; she is also a spiritualist. She holds seances; she has been in touch with the spirits of the dead. She has talked with Kingsford-Smith's departed spirit and can tell you in exactly which inaccessible part of the Blue Mountains his plane has crashed.

She lends me books, which I read in bed with Jennie when she comes home on Saturday nights. They give very matter-of-fact accounts of all sorts of ghosts: some who appear to answer your perplexities, some who have committed crimes and need to confess, some who have been murdered and want to tell the truth about their deaths. One is a little girl ghost I can relate to, who just comes and sits on the end of the bed, wanting someone to talk to. We read these stories till the small hours and are so disturbed by them that we have to hold hands and run and turn off the light together.

I return the books. I make a firm rational decision that I have too much trouble coping with the real people in my life to start worrying about ghosts, and deal with them with academic rigour when they crop up in essays.

From time to time I long to escape from the difficulties of higher learning and return to the certainties and simplicities of romances and murders, of sheriffs and rustlers, where the goodies are good and the baddies are bad, the baddies get caught, the woman gets her man, and the hero is always strong, silent and heroic.

But alas! I am hooked on the complexities of the great characters of history and literature.

It is Auntie Doll, my old ally, who provides a bridge.

She is now very old and so disabled by arthritis that she can hardly hobble from room to room. Her two hands have become hideous claws, and she now can't even hold the cards for the bridge game that has been her weekly pleasure for many years. I never hear her complain, and when I ask about the pain, she says, shaking her head and clicking her tongue: 'It's not too bad, till it gets near time for the next dose of aspirin.' And she changes the subject.

From her I borrow books, best-sellers of the day, like Galsworthy's *Forsyte Saga* and Mazo de la Roche's *Jalna* books, and the books in these series supply a need for me, in that the characters in one book are also the characters in the next book, not with the same emphasis or importance, but still there, still breathing and talking, developing well or badly, and I find this very satisfying and unlike life as I know it, in which people come and go, or go and never come back, or went and came back so terrifyingly changed that you could never be sure that they were the same people you remembered.

Or even worse, you could never be sure that they were not.

We go one night to Grandmother's, where Auntie still lives. I don't know why we have come so late in the evening — perhaps Daddy has come to 'borrow' some money from Grandmother. Certainly he isn't in the sitting room, and Mother has stayed home for some reason. Auntie is sitting on a hassock, huddled down with her ear close to the big old console wireless, and tears are rolling down her cheeks.

'That was Artur Schnabel playing that piece,' she

says. 'Mozart. I used to play that piece myself, and when I listen to him, I know that I played it well, too.'

Daddy comes into the room and she quickly collects herself, and says briskly: 'And how's your Mother, dear?'

Home in bed that night I remember Auntie's crying. She is the only grown-up I have ever seen cry quietly.

And I wish I could do something like play the piano, that would stir me so deeply and with such remembered pleasure. Perhaps I could write a book?

I start by writing a piece for the school magazine. It is published, on nice shiny paper like a real book. I take it home (the first thing I have taken home since the gold medal), and the others read it, without seeing anything to get excited about. Daddy hears about it. 'Show me what you've written,' he says, and though he just reads it through and gives it back, he stares at me as though he's seen something that I'd missed, so that I panic. Writing! I must never do that again!

A few days after the Mozart episode with Auntie, we study Keats' 'Ode to a Nightingale', whose song 'Charmed magic casements, opening on the foam / Of perilous seas, in faery lands forlorn', and into my head float the beautiful clear notes of a piano, without me understanding at all what it means to me.

Our history teacher takes us into the hall one day and talks about the retreat from Moscow and plays for us the 1812 overture, and for the third time that week the music stirs some deep memory in me, and I see an old type of gramophone, with a big trumpet for a speaker, like the picture on the record label of a dog listening to 'His Master's Voice'. And I become one of Napoleon's soldiers dying of hunger and cold in the icy wastes of Russia in 1812.

I begin to be full of anxiety, as though the music is opening doors I would rather stayed shut.

I am one Pandora who is opening no boxes!

OUT OF THE CHRYSALIS

Up TILL now, under cover of my school uniform, I have merged into the scene at school, feeling pretty much equal in many respects and better than equal in others.

But towards the end of that final year the feeling that I am not like other girls follows me to school, and as I look around at what they are doing this year, I know that it is true. I am not into clothes and make-up and dances and riding in cars with boys; I am into reading and studying and the choir.

All the music in the school is in the hands of the only man on the staff, who also directs the choir. I have been in the choir for two years, and the songs we sing there are as different from the hit parade songs that I know off by heart as Shakespeare and Hardy and Milton and Virgil are from the murders and romances and wild west books of my younger days.

We sing old songs, madrigals, Shakespearean songs, *It Was a Lover and his Lass,* old part songs, a bit of *The New World Symphony* put to words, old weird ballads. It has been a whole new wonderful world opening up for me. But I resign from the choir in that last year. I claim pressure of work, but it has something to do also with the music, and the fact that the choir-master starts putting his ear close to our mouths to listen as we sing. I do not yet know déjà vu, but I have the unsettling feeling that this has happened to me before, and though he says nothing, I am frightened by his listening, and it seems better to resign before I am put out.

I start listening to more general conversations and now, suddenly, they are all about boys.

Some of the girls tell great giggling tales of wild times at dances on Saturday nights with beer and cigarettes, and boys and girls going out of the dance into the bushes, and my transparent face probably shows what I am thinking — that this is not what I want.

My own friends are swots like myself, but they too have a life they can talk about outside school.

One friend, Catherine, is being teased one day by the others because she has been seen at church with a boy, and suddenly, with one of the old-type flashes that alarm me so, I see her there, clearly, and she is wearing a beautiful blue dress with a satin collar, and her blonde hair, instead of being disciplined into a neat plait as it always is at school, is flowing about her in curls. Her face is aglow.

Margaret, another close friend (if anyone could be close to someone who never talks about what goes on outside school), has had a boyfriend for years, and they go out to the beach, and to movies, and to dances, and she talks about petting in his car afterwards, always stopping short, she assures me, of you-know-what. (Imagine having a boyfriend with a car!) She tells me they are to marry one year after she has finished school.

Even Angela gets a boyfriend and talks about him starry-eyed when we are alone.

I am relieved that no-one can see what my life is like outside school. It has no such pleasures as other girls are describing, and I can see no prospect of it changing. I haven't even talked to a boy since the day I cried at central school after Harry went west, and was labelled queer. I decide it is time I overcame this serious flaw (serious, but not fatal, I hope!) in my character. I start by making eyes at a man I meet every morning in St Kilda Road as I walk to school, and he stops and chats to me and invites me to go swimming with him to the Malvern Baths on Saturday afternoon.

I panic and stammer: 'My father wouldn't let me!' After that I walk on the other side of St Kilda Road.

I am simply too frightened.

A month before I finish school, my father takes me skating, after a conversation overheard, like many of the important conversations in my life, when I'm not supposed to be listening.

'For God's sake,' my mother is saying, 'take her somewhere she'll meet some boys, or we'll never get her off our hands!'

'It's those books!' my father says in a fury. 'All she thinks about is those bloody books! It's not natural! She's got her head in the clouds! And it's that bloody school she goes to — nothing but girls and a lot of old maids.'

So here I am, one Saturday afternoon at the skating rink, wearing a pair of hired skates and clinging in desperation to a rail in mugs' alley. I watch my father's retreating back as he heads for the nearest pub where he can have a beer in peace and listen to the races on the wireless.

I have a moment's panic. I have hardly gone anywhere alone since second form when I used to wag it from school and go to the movies and escape into worlds where I thought no-one could follow.

Something of that feeling invades me now that my father has gone. There's nobody here who knows me, so it doesn't matter if I make a fool of myself. It can't get worse — it can only get better.

So I start my first voyage of exploration alone.

I look round at the other girls in the rink. They are all wearing little flared skating skirts and beautiful jackets with decorations on them, and their make-up and hair stay just so no matter what gyrations they perform. Their boots are not hired, but match their skirts, and they skate in them as though they have been born in them, with an easy, effortless grace.

What I feel as I look at them is too deep for mere envy; it is more like a deep shame that I am so different.

'What am I doing here?' I mourn, and I echo Mother's words: 'Why can't you be more like other girls?'

I look at the boys. Certainly there are plenty of boys, and I understand that boys are a necessity if you are to avoid the old-maid status. Some are skating in circles or figure eights, or performing other amazing feats like the lords of creation. Others are fast skating, racing round the rink and leaping in the air and down again with an air of such intense ferocity that I cling to my rail in terror, and the air around me is filled with bleeding fingers, noses, legs or arms severed by those flashing blades.

In my panic my own blunt blades slide from under me, and I clutch at whatever is nearest and that is the crutch of a nearby, equally unsteady, young man, and we both come down hard and wet on the ice. I know I shouldn't laugh, but it comes out anyway, first in a surreptitious trickle, then in a flood.

It has always been one of the worst measures of my difference that when a situation is too fraught with risk for tears or apologies, when any sensible person would know that it is time to shut up, I may become convulsed with laughter.

But the enemy, whom I have possibly disabled, is laughing too.

'Pretty girl!' his eyes say, and he doesn't even seem to notice how dumb and awkward I am or that my clothes don't fit and that now I am wet, my hair is hanging down limply.

He helps me up and suggests we go round together.

'I'm hopeless,' he says, and he laughs and doesn't care, and soon I am laughing and not caring too.

So we skate jerkily off, managing to stay, well, nearly upright, and to laugh and talk at the same time, and we go round and round until it becomes easy. Whatever I am babbling about makes him laugh, and he calls me 'Miss Originality'.

And after what seems like a very short time he takes me back to the rail where, breathless but perfectly balanced and warm, we look into each other's eyes with joy and excitement — magic, it is.

Cinderella never had it so good.

And just as he is saying: 'When can I —' my eyes are drawn to the seats and tables at the side, where my father stands, imperiously beckoning.

It is suddenly midnight, and I am the girl in my sister's cast-off dress with the row of tucks not quite under my breasts, and the hired skates with the cast-iron blades.

Real life beckons, and in real life there are no princes, only duty and hard work and the family, and magic is strictly for the fairy stories.

'Goodbye,' I say to him and stagger back to the rail and the exit, leaving him, above all, amazed.

Things get bad.

My wisdom teeth come through decayed — is it an omen? I go to the free dental hospital where an inexperienced undergraduate yanks vainly at my tooth, finally putting his knee in my chest to give him the necessary leverage for the extraction. I glare at him, and if looks could kill, there would have been one less dentist to graduate that year. He excavates the rotting stumps without benefit of anaesthetic. I decide if you have no money, you're not supposed to have feelings.

I go home and treat myself to a fortnight in bed with influenza, and feel like dying.

The school camp looms up. This year it is to be at Phillip Island, but it has nothing to do with me; I have never been and I don't even think about it. But Margaret is called up to the head's office and pumped about my home life. They want to know would I like to go to the camp? They have noticed that I seem — well, not quite myself, and not well. With the final external exams coming up, perhaps a holiday would be good for me. Margaret is no help; she simply doesn't know. They send her off to sound me out as to how I'd feel about going.

'I don't know! My father wouldn't let me!' I say and I am close to breaking.

But what flash into my mind are Catherine's dress with the satin collar and the only other dress beside my school tunic that I own, the hand-me-down from Jennie that I wore skating.

I am summoned down to the office and asked if I would like to go; there would be no charge, the school was paying. They have ordered — reading my mind? using their eyes and their commonsense? — from Myers' Emporium two dresses in my size, girlish and charming and suitable for my colouring. I try them on in the headmistress's office, exposing my grubby singlet and my raggy pants, and I begin to cry.

To my deep shame, I begin to cry, in front of the principal and the vice-principal and my friend the history teacher, without quite knowing what I am crying for, except that this is charity, and up till now, because of the scholarship, I had felt safe from that at high school. It is all spoilt.

But I go home and ask, and after the usual amount of interrogation and roaring, I go on the camp with my two new dresses and a beautiful pink woollen one with a cross-over bodice, gift of the caretaking aunt. In it I feel very sophisticated, but I get unspoken messages from the staff that it is — well, not quite suitable.

Camp is an experience. I am put in a room with four other girls, three of them the drinkers and smokers. I don't sleep very well, but in a limited way I enjoy myself. I wear one of the new dresses every day in turn, which is in itself a joy. I go to my first barbecue. I eat a sausage on a stick. I play parlour games. I go for walks along wild cliffs with the sea roaring, exciting and menacing, below. Thank God it is too cold to swim! Nobody is mean to me.

I come home two weeks later, reluctantly, to Mother, who senses my mood.

'Well, you'd better get out of those clothes and come back to earth. We can't all be out enjoying ourselves all day.'

The final disaster for the year comes after the final assembly, which I, along with several other truants, have skipped in favour of a gossip in the prefects' room.

Rhoda rushes in. 'Congratulations!' she says to me. I am relieved. I know what she is talking about. I have worked it out that I should get the Proxime Accessit prize, awarded to the pupil who comes second in her final year. But then Rhoda rushes over to another girl. 'Congratulations!' she says. 'You've won the Proxime Accessit!'

I am devastated. 'But . . . but . . . you said . . .'

No, no. Rhoda was congratulating me on being *dux of the school*.

I've done it again. Why does everything have to happen twice?

Speech night. In the Melbourne Town Hall. Mother and Daddy in the audience, Mother purring a little, Daddy glowering. I have to go up on the stage, decked in the obligatory white dress (ghastly) which Mother has scrounged from somewhere, and receive words of praise and two leather-bound volumes with my name printed in beautiful antique writing on the fly-leaf, so again there is no mistake. I know that with the best will in the world I could hardly have copied the reams of tests and essays and exam papers that have brought me to this.

The secret is out: that I am good at school, that I have done something better than Daddy, that I am not stupid. It is a secret I can't keep any longer.

And I am still alive.

BLACKWOOD

EVERYONE'S GLAD when the letter comes.

Since the exams finished, for three weeks I have done nothing but sleep. I sleep all night till late in the morning. I get up and do a few mechanical chores and after that I sleep again. The others come home from work and we have tea, but I am already yawning and ready for bed again.

My school uniform is in the rubbish bin; my two new dresses hang in the wardrobe, too good to wear except out, and I never go out, so I dag around the house in an old dress of Jennie's and feel like death warmed up. I float on a sea of emptiness with no rudder to steer by and the lights of no safe port to head for.

Two fitful lights gleam weakly in the distance.

The first is the possibility of a course at university, which depends on my external exam results, and I am not too hopeful. I remember making some stupid mistakes in those exams. The staff at school had told me that if I did well I should get a government scholarship, but the man who's been financing Daddy in his latest venture has a son finishing school at Melbourne Grammar, and he has assured Daddy that government scholarships go only to pupils of private schools who've been doing matriculation for two years. As soon as I walked into the Exhibition building where the external examinations were held, I could see he was right. There were a few girls there, and a lot of boys from Melbourne Boys' High, but the hall was mainly full of boys wearing the regalia of the exclusive private schools. So there's little hope — or fear — of me getting a scholarship.

I'm not even sure that I want to go to university. I've read in some Middle Ages history book a wonderful account of Oxford as a place where poor students sat at the feet of wise masters and were guided in discussions on literature and philosophy — a place where you could *talk*.

This hopeful version is overlaid by a recent page from *Truth*, torn from the wrappings around Friday night's fish and chips and read in stealth later. This scandal sheet is taboo in our family, but Daddy sometimes buys it for the racing tips, and we usually manage to scrounge it and read the juiciest bits when Mother has secretly finished with it. In the fish-and-chips version, University Dons (are they teachers or students?) are dashing good-looking fellows with fast cars and loose ways with women. Both these pictures have a certain scary charm.

The other dim light is provided by a meeting scheduled for mid-January with a group of school inspectors who will interview me to determine whether I am a fit person to teach primary school pupils.

Memories of Mrs McPhee from primary school, who rescued me from the clutches of the headmaster, tilt me towards the teaching job. It would involve leaving home! I would get paid for it. Perhaps I would have a boyfriend, something I would never dare at home.

It is at this point that the letter comes. It is addressed to me, but Mother and Daddy have of course opened it, discussed it, and decided I am to go, so there's no decision required from me. I think everyone is as pleased as I am when I read it at the prospect of such a misery-guts being away for two weeks.

The letter is from Uncle Don, 'Nature's gentleman'. They have heard about me being dux of the school and wonder if I would like to spend a couple of weeks with them and some friends in a place they rent every year at Blackwood.

So here I am, with my bag packed, being driven by Daddy to what turns out to be an old mining town, consisting of a lot of little single-fronted cottages, mostly now decaying and deserted, a wooden pub with a veranda with seats all round and a general store.

Daddy and Uncle Don greet each other circumspectly, and Uncle starts visibly when he sees me. I am not the little girl he remembers. I am now seventeen, and wearing one of the caretaking aunt's dresses, a blue voile with a ruffled organdie collar. It fits me almost too well. I have lost two stone in the last year, what with flu and anxiety and teeth and examinations, and blue suits me. Three weeks of doing nothing but eat and sleep have probably helped, and even I know that I have a good figure.

So it is with some misgivings that Uncle introduces me to his friend's son, John, who has also just finished high school, though without the mix of glory and consternation of my own last year. John's mother ('Call me Irene', an unheard-of liberty with grown-ups) is not at all alarmed; she is kind and friendly, and tells John to take me for a walk in the bush while she gets tea.

As soon as I am alone with him, I am suddenly so nervous I can hardly speak, and compensate for this by babbling incoherently and incidentally showing an unsuitable amount of botanical knowledge about the Australian bush. He delivers me home to his mother as soon as he decently can, and confides to her (as she tells me later) that I'm far too clever for him.

As well as John there are two other boys of my own age, and apparently no other girls in the district, and we four become almost inseparable. I seem to be accepted as part of the group — even John seems to have forgiven me for being dux of the school and too clever by half, and tells his mother that 'Emma's nice, when you get to know her'. I go where they go, and none of them tries to separate me off from the others; we just walk and talk, and sit and talk, and I ride on the back of Ray's motorbike, and the other two ride their push-bikes, and we talk and explore the countryside. We just like each other. They do most of the talking and I listen, and that to me is fascinating. I don't have to show my knowledge or hide it, and like the girls at school, they don't ask me any embarrassing questions about home or expect me to say much, and because their lives are so different from mine their stories are interesting to me.

John is a student at Melbourne Boys' High, the brother school to MacRob, but he makes no chocolate-factory jokes, so it is all right. Depending on his results he may go back to school for a second year, and this uncertainty does not seem to worry him at all.

Tony works as a glassblower; he tells us about blowing the glass into glasses and vases and animals. It is a job you only do for ten years because it affects your lungs. He too does not seem alarmed by the uncertainty.

Ray is the one with the motorbike. He is over six feet tall, and works as a motor mechanic at Trentham, nearby. He is easy to talk to, and is — or seems — a lot older, almost a man, while the other two are just boys.

On Friday morning when I walk into the kitchen they are all talking about the dance.

They're so busy talking they don't even notice me come in. Irene and Don's wife, Jess, are planning the cakes they will make for supper. John is told to ride to a nearby farm to get fresh cream and eggs. Don and his friend Alex have to borrow extra chairs to set around the wall of the hall, and to be ready to meet the musicians who will arrive from Melbourne by bus. They are also on the committee that's going to oversee the behaviour of the young, especially those from neighbouring districts who will be bringing beer. (There's no policeman for miles around.) Nobody asks me to come, but when I go off with the boys, I understand why.

Everybody goes. You don't have to be invited. Panic!

'I can't go,' I say. 'I can't dance!'

They just brush it off.

'Everyone goes!' they say.

So on Saturday night I dress in my least attractive dress (courtesy of the caretaking aunt), a stiff checked taffeta, which I've chosen because Jennie has said it's for evening wear. Irene suggests tactfully that the blue voile might be better, but I'm too uptight to change, and terribly anxious for once to be wearing the right thing. Dances — boys — alcohol — the bushes — and the last night at school when I went to my only dance, and all the girls in the matriculation class danced with each other, me in a borrowed slinky green dress with a slit skirt which even I knew was unsuitable and in which I could hardly move. Ugh!

The boys take me and I abandon them at the door and head for the chairs by the wall, prepared to be, like the girl in *Getting of Wisdom*, a wallflower for the night. The music has already started, and whenever anyone asks me to dance, I shake my head and mutter: 'I can't dance.'

But an older man comes over and refuses to take no for an answer; he says simply: 'Everyone can dance,' and whisks me away. He shows me the basic steps of a simple dance, and before I know what is happening, I am dancing, and it is terrifying and exciting and exhilarating, and the man and I are swept away in the music and the dance. It is like skating — once you start doing it, it's as though you knew all the time; you have known it for centuries, for thousands of years; it is in your blood, in your bones, and it just needed someone to touch the spring to awaken it all.

I suppose I must have danced with others, eaten supper, walked home with the boys, but the rest is a blur.

I fall into bed, and next day two things happen to bring me back to earth.

The first is that Ray and I go out for a walk alone together, the other two having gone in to Trentham to get some new tyres for Tony's bike. We just walk and talk, and it is so pleasant in his company that everything else recedes, and when we get tired, we sit together on the rotting front veranda of a little old cottage, deserted and beginning to fall apart, and we talk some more. Ray gives me my first cigarette, which makes me cough and splutter, and we laugh, and Ray says, 'If you don't like it, don't smoke it,' and I put it out.

We start to get hungry and head for home, still talking.

A hundred yards from home we spot a pathetic figure. It is Uncle. He is wringing his hands and groaning: 'What would your father say?' He takes out his gold watch and points to it. 'Look at the time! A quarter to nine! We've been worried sick about you!'

What have I done? What did I do? It is still broad summer daylight — there is no need for all this fuss! I remember the cigarette and feel vaguely guilty — but not guilty of what Uncle evidently suspects me of. Inside I realise the alarm has been compounded by a telegram that has been sitting on the sideboard all afternoon — even Irene has been worried. Telegrams are always and only portents of death or disaster.

CONGRATULATIONS! FIRST CLASS HONOURS ENGLISH LATIN EUROPEAN HISTORY SECOND HONOURS FRENCH STOP SENIOR GOVERNMENT SCHOLARSHIP STOP EXHIBITION TO TRINITY COLLEGE STOP.

I pass it over. Irene is delighted. She kisses me! She means it! Uncle is mollified. John is impressed. I am only enraged — but trying not to show it.

Why does *he* always have to butt in when I'm enjoying myself? For twelve whole wonderful days I have forgotten his very existence — and now this! They were *my* results and I'd wanted to see them first! He'd only sent that telegram to impress Uncle and Auntie with what a good fellow he is!

But I pull myself together and Irene produces a bottle of lovely fizzy champagne and they all drink to my success; Uncle's colour subsides to a safer level and I try to pretend that nothing has changed.

When I am home again, Tony comes round with a big batch of photos taken at Blackwood with his box Brownie camera, but I don't even feel like the same girl as the happy relaxed girl with the ruffled collar in the photos. I am only anxious to get rid of Tony before

Daddy comes home and realises I've been talking — talking to boys, talking to strangers, saying heaven knows what. Even the thought that he had only congratulated me to impress the others now seems wicked and dangerous.

I never see any of the boys or Uncle Don again, and I have the feeling that it is all my fault, but nothing can take it away from me, those twelve days when I was just like everybody else and knew it was possible just to be happy without even thinking about it.

UNIVERSITY

I HAVE been invited out to afternoon tea with Miss Lehmann. I am dressed in a beautifully cut dress simply made of some knobbly material, which fits me perfectly and which has been given by the caretaking aunt, not to Jennie this time, but to me. I feel quite grand.

The feeling doesn't last.

It's the starched white cloths and the gleaming silverware and the flowers on the tables, like something out of an old bad dream, that get to me first, then the waitress with her frilly apron who comes to take our order, and the groups of well-dressed people sitting at the tables talking seriously or pleasantly — all this adds up to yet another new world in which I do not know how to behave. What if I spill my tea or slop something on my dress?

I don't, but Miss Lehmann does — she knocks over her cup and tea flows everywhere, over the starched cloth, over the cutlery, even onto the carpet. She is totally unconcerned, she signals to the waitress who mops up pleasantly with a minimum of fuss, as though spilling your tea was the most natural thing in the world.

(Such calm! Such aplomb! Is this what the real world, in which my father is convinced I'll be eaten alive, is like?)

Miss Lehmann is dressed in something nicer than I have ever seen her in. First she congratulates me on my results, my scholarship, then she gets down to business with her usual efficiency and begins to talk about university. She takes it for granted I will be going, and that it is wonderful. She is as concise and explicit as she was in history lessons as she explains exactly what a government scholarship provides: forty pounds a year, which will cover fees, books and union fees, but nothing else. Then she dives in off the deep end. Will my family be able to afford clothes for me? She eyes the expensive dress, perhaps remembering those ghastly underclothes. I say yes and mean no, and she goes quickly on. She and the principal and the vice-principal have been having a chat and would like to lend me a little money — say ten shillings a week — till I graduate in three years' time. This would enable me to join more fully in university life. It would just be a loan, she says quickly, possibly anxious to avoid a repeat of the school trip scene, and I could pay it back a little every week when I am through my course and have a job.

Ten shillings a week! For myself! What would I do with such unheard-of riches?

'There'll be a lot of little expenses connected with being at university,' she tells me, as if she has read my thoughts. 'You'll be able to take part in university life a lot better if you have a little money.'

I am amazed that anyone would trust me enough to lend me money without security (I know about such things since the bankruptcy) and am relieved that I am to be still connected with the school where I have felt so secure. And the fact that three teachers have cared enough to offer it, even though I am not a relation and no longer even their responsibility as a student, makes me feel as though I still matter. Yet I have for a long time felt ashamed at being the only one who has not contributed to the family finances, and I don't think I can go on sponging on them for another three years.

Daddy listens without comment to my story when I go home, but makes no comment except a predictable mutter about people interfering between a man and his children. Surprisingly Daddy is in favour of me going to university. (Anything to keep me under his thumb a bit longer?) I hear him instructing Mother: 'Try and talk her into it. It'll keep her out of mischief for another three years.'

When it is decided, he comes back to my cousins Kenneth and Alice.

'Your uncle kept a little book, and in it he wrote down every penny he'd spent on their education, and they had to pay it back when they grew up and started earning.'

I don't remember my father spending anything on my education except a few exercise books, but I have probably eaten a mountain of food in my time, as well as train fares and shoes and some clothes. All this was certainly not covered by the few vacation jobs I had, so it will probably take the rest of my life to pay it all back. And now this!

Like so much of my life, it doesn't bear thinking about!

Hopes of a primary school job have petered out after the interview with the school inspectors.

We have been briefed about the routine for this at school: Go up to the panel, introduce yourself and, when called, tell a story of your choice to a class of preppies, then you will be interviewed by the inspectors. I arrive in good time, well scrubbed, to be pounced on by Cicely from school, whom I've always considered a bit of a drip. Her story, she tells me proudly, is to be about Tannhauser.

'Hell!' I think. 'Who or what is Tannhauser?' and my Three Bears suddenly seems stupid and babyish. The preppies don't notice, however, they lap it up with rapt attention so that we don't even notice that the two inspectors who have been watching and assessing have drifted out in the middle.

As for the interview, they ask me only one question: 'How did you get on in the external examinations?' When I tell them, they just look at each other and laugh.

'We don't need to worry about her!' they say to each other. 'She'll get a scholarship and be off to university!'

And they bow me out.

('Oh! Mrs MacPhee! I didn't make it!')

So here I am, bumbling my way round the University of Melbourne — the *only* Victorian university — a vast sprawling place with many buildings, some beautiful old buildings like medieval churches, some glaringly modern, dotted all over it among lawns and paths, and a little lane called Tin Alley on which cars could drive, and even a lake with a few seedy-looking ducks swimming on it. Guided by signposts, I make it at last into the Registrar's office and do a repeat-after-me, promising 'to respectfully submit to the constituted authorities', sign the matriculation book and totter away to meet a couple of girls from school whom I've never liked much but whom I cling to at first as if to a life raft.

At first it is like a repeat of high school. I concentrate on not being noticed, merge invisibly with the priests and nuns in Latin classes, am swallowed up with hundreds of well-dressed self-confident boys and girls in the vast English lecture theatre, or with a silent throng in French lectures.

It is not hard to be invisible here. They mark no rolls, and nobody seems to know or care whether you're there or not, so I attend those lectures where the lecturer does not seem too threatening and seems to love his subject and want to share his pleasure with us, and I skip the rest. I spend long wicked hours in the library, reading books not on the curriculum, some of them only half understood — extra Elizabethan drama, Irish playwrights (probably from beyond the pale) and dip into all sorts of books that other people have left lying about on the library tables.

I spend more wicked hours drinking coffee in the 'caf', contributing little but listening well to conversations with girls doing science and medicine, as well as those doing arts, which is rather despised by those in other faculties.

One set of tutorials I attend regularly: those at Trinity. I have recovered from my fear that they will throw me out when they find I am not C. of E. and enjoy the comparative intimacy of nine boys and two girls working with a tutor. We translate into Latin bits of English prose of such erudition that it is sometimes as much of a problem to understand the English as to translate it into Latin. We torture the Latin language into halting hexameters. Together we translate parts of Tacitus' histories and sometimes rather bawdy bits of Plautus. Sometimes we even laugh and talk. A clergyman's son translates *concubina* as *girlfriend* and our tutor snorts, breaking the word up into its parts: '*Con-cubina! Con = with! Cubina = bed! Woman what sleeps with!*', and it is safe to laugh with everyone else and I feel part of a very select group.

French tutorials — fifteen minutes alone with a French speaker — are more than I can bear, and I skip the lot.

It all catches up with me at the end of the year. Part of the French exam is a conversation session, with a M. Karagheusian, a short, fat, bald, olive-skinned man, very alive and forceful. He shows his teeth and his feelings in a very uninhibited way. '*Qui êtes-vous?*' he fires at me, when I go into his study for the test.

'Who are you?'

'Where do you come from?'

'Why have I not seen you before? You should have been here once each week all year. Where have you been?'

I mumble in my schoolgirl French (we'd read it and written it at school, but almost never spoken it, and I have only got through at university because I have *an ear* and can understand what the French speakers are saying) that I have taken French conversation at Trinity with M. Canard. At this lie I blush scarlet and begin to sweat so profusely that he knows it is not true. I'm sure I'm not the first (though surely the most incompetent) lying undergraduate he has had to deal with, and he breaks out into a great belly laugh of pure amusement, spreads out his hands and says: '*Et maintenant! Vous êtes ici!*' and he begins to talk. I feel a gush of pure love for him at such generosity, and we begin to have a conversation, me groping at first for the right words but responding to what this skilled conversationalist gives me with such pleasure that I soon begin to get the right words and almost the right pronunciation.

I get a 3H in French when I should have got at least a second, but it is survival. After this close shave I take myself in hand and realise that if I'm to get this degree and the job that will bring freedom, I must start going to lectures and working as seriously and systematically as I did at school. And I begin to enjoy it again.

I still enjoy sneaking off to avant-garde French films at the Russell Street cinema, where they show continental films with sub-titles (these are no hardship to me, brought up on silent films) and serve you biscuits and tea in the interval. I still enjoy the illicit reading in the silence and peace of the library, and the missed lectures and the lectures I go to, and the largely uncensored conversations at Trinity and in the 'caf'. I have the same feeling in a much more limited way that I used to have at school, that as long as I do the work and 'submit respectfully to the constituted authorities' (and nobody ever gives me any orders to obey), and as long as nobody at home knows what I am up to, I have a sort of freedom.

Having some money of my own is part of this; perhaps the first stone in the edifice of my independence. My ten shillings a week has shrunk from being untold wealth to being difficult to manage on, but it keeps me in lengths of material that I make up into sometimes quite successful dresses, in cups of coffee and lipstick, an occasional tram ride to town if the weather is too frightful, and in service-weight nylons that have to last a month whether they have laddered or not.

My friend Mary goes to celebrity concerts wearing a wonderful green and silver lamé evening coat her mother has bought her, and has an account at Georges and another at Myers, where she buys the best brands of shoes two pairs at a time. I must surely have been envious, but I felt about it the way I'd felt about the annual camp at school — that because I don't have any money, these things do not apply to me. The boys who reside in Trinity wear beautiful Harris tweed jackets, some with leather patches on their elbows, such as my father and brothers have never even dreamt of. The non-resident boys wear serviceable navy or grey suits, increasingly threadbare and shiny as we approach the end of our three-year course. But nobody seems to care what we wear — or so I imagine. I am often more uneasy in the occasional high-fashion dress from the caretaking aunt than in the homemade dresses and hand-knitted jumpers that I usually wear.

But here, as at school, everybody has a life outside university. They talk about celebrity concerts and theatres or overseas trips or the races or family parties — none of this is happening in my life.

I go to university plays in which my friends perform, and I envy them but don't have the guts to go to the casting meetings. I go to university revues, and feel I ought to be shocked by the entertaining goings-on on stage, but never am. I am taken by friends to a play at Queens, and stay too late for the last train, and am in agony till a boy offers to drive me home; I go to *French Without Tears* and other films with boys and it is all quite pleasant, but there is none of the drama and excitement of Jennie's string of boyfriends. That, I feel, cannot happen till I can leave home.

I have braced myself for that to happen after three years, but at the end of the third year my scholarship runs out, and the Education Department will not employ me without a Diploma of Education. Instead, they offer me a studentship for the year, but if I accept

I must sign a bond promising (swearing?) to teach for three and a half years after I get the diploma. By then I will be almost an old lady, and nobody will want me!

The principal from school writes, asking me to call.

They will not be able to pay me the usual ten shillings a week once I graduate. They have another student in need of help. I am desolate, almost as much at this final cutting of the tie, the loss of my sense of belonging, as with the loss of the money.

I have to make a decision — never an easy thing for me. But the me that decided after Harry went west that I was going to be a teacher takes over. I am interviewed, but before I can sign the bond, people start dying.

PEOPLE START DYING

IN MY final year of arts, though I go home every night from university, I am somehow more detached from it all, from the rows (mainly between Jock and Daddy, these days), from the now less frequent moving from house to house and from suburb to suburb, from Jock's changing jobs and Jennie's changing boyfriends, from Mother's asthma, her illnesses, her operations, her bad back and her phlebitis.

In an effort to find some kind of social life outside the family, Jennie, Jock and I start going to church and join the young people's group, the Christian Endeavour. At first we arouse considerable antagonism, because we stick so closely together that it's hard for anyone to 'get in' with any of us, but that passes, and soon Jennie and Jock have signed a form giving their hearts to Jesus, but I hang back.

I have always had trouble with God. It is surprising how largely he figured in my imagination, considering the sketchiness of my religious education — being hounded off to Sunday school occasionally in the vain hope that it would make me a better girl. Later I wondered if it was so they could have sex in peace on Sunday morning with no kids around? But early on, my difficulty was that God seemed so like Daddy in many ways.

It wasn't safe to say anything against him.

He lost me completely when I learned that he had made Abraham stand over Isaac with a knife to prove something or other.

He gave up his only begotten son to suffer and die for the sins of the world. (Was Jesus told that it was all his fault, that he should never have been born?) I have a sense that it was rather morbid and masochistic of Jesus to want to die for the sins of others (but perhaps he felt he had no choice?).

I don't want to die for someone else's sins and I certainly don't want anyone dying for mine. And although I don't believe in him, I am secretly very angry with God for giving up his only beloved son for such a purpose. Sons don't seem to be very safe around God.

Another way in which God seemed like Daddy was that he was a thrower-out. He threw Adam and Eve out of the garden of Eden for no other reason than that they knew — or wanted to know — too much, which put me very much at risk with him.

As well, God blamed the woman. Adam, of course, was a good boy — he didn't even like apples! He would never have done such a wicked thing if she hadn't made him!

But most of all, he was so scary. If you told a lie, or took his name in vain (whatever that meant!), he could strike you dead. I was very afraid of being struck dead by someone you were supposed to love but couldn't.

The main things that keep me going to church are the music — there is a good choir that sings Handel — and perhaps some dim feeling that even I might be acceptable to Jesus.

On Sundays, we are preached at about the evils of drink — as a Rechabite I am safe there — and of getting into bad (i.e. un-Christian) company. And although the actual word 'sex' is never mentioned, we are warned about the evils of dancing. This is demonstrated by one leader taking a group to the Arts Ball in the city to witness horrid scenes of drunkenness and unspecified depravity. I don't go. Somehow I don't think I need an Arts Ball.

Jock falls sort-of in love with a slinky brunette who goes to church, and Jennie with a nice man called Bert who I would have liked for myself, but I realise I have no chance against Jennie, she being the eldest, so I settle for a limited attachment to a boy called Billy, whom I like and admire, but shrink from his sincere attachment to both the church and his slightly ferocious mother.

Daddy has been managing two grocery shops, financed by the man whose son was at Melbourne Grammar.

But he has done his dough. The businesses both go bust — the banks again! Nothing to do with the fact that blocks of unrefrigerated butter were likely to slide oilily onto the floor on some hot night, or that his kids helped themselves freely to chocolate royal biscuits or anything else on the shelves that was edible or palatable, or that his car would break down so that he could not deliver the weekend groceries to some family that was depending on them.

In the vacation, Billy's mother asks me to stay and help her with the housework for a week when she is bedridden. I agree with some trepidation, both because I am regarded as totally incompetent in this area, and because of the row with Jennie when she went as a maid. However, Daddy is as unpredictable as ever. He just asks whether I got paid, and I hand it over.

Billy's mother is one of his grocery shop customers, and he has to deliver her last order. He turns on the charm. He explains how he (who never gave anyone a penny of credit in his life) is owed more by his customers than he owes to the bank. He is, of course, the wronged one.

Billy's mother repeats all this to me sadly.

'Your poor father!' she says. 'And he's such a lovely man! I could weep for him!'

I just stare. It's no use saying anything, because the reaction is always the same. He is the wronged one. Nobody would ever believe me if I told the truth. Forget it!

And I think, as I have thought a hundred times before: it's hopeless! It's no use telling anyone — not the policeman, not Mother, not any other woman —

what he has done, because the reaction is always the same! He is the good one. He is the lovely man who wouldn't hurt a fly. If I tell, they will lock me up and throw away the key! Forget it!

It is another nail in my coffin.

Before the year is out, both Bert and Billy are married to other girls (I am bridesmaid to Billy's bride), and Jock has joined the army. I farewell him at the train and as no other member of the family is present, I weep buckets, convinced that I will never see him again.

'Women love to cry,' he says gruffly to Billy and his fiancée, who are also farewelling him, and I am once again ashamed of my tears.

Jennie's visits become less and less frequent. She soon has a new beau, a suitor of rather different calibre. I hear a lot about Paul from Jennie in the three weeks before I meet him. He is English, many years older than Jennie. He was nearly chosen to play rugby for England. His mother was a matriarch, his father rich but disapproving. 'I'm a kind of remittance man,' he tells us cheerfully, but that is much later, when he has been accepted into the bosom of the family. I find this disarming; in our family no-one would dream of making such an unflattering remark about him or herself.

'He's coming to the flat tonight for dinner,' says Jennie. (It was always 'tea' before Paul showed up.) 'He's promised to bring fromage. What's fromage, Emma?'

I may cut no ice at the Melbourne University School of French, but at home I am still the resident expert.

I first meet Paul one cold wet dreary day at the registry office, where Jennie has asked me to meet her so I can be a witness to her wedding.

'You're the only one I can trust not to put a stop to it,' she says, and I wonder whether I should be putting a stop to it, but know I can't. Jennie seems much better at doing what she wants than I am. So I am the sole witness as an uninterested public servant in a bare bleak office mumbles a few toneless words about loving and honouring and obeying; Jennie and Paul repeat them after him and they are married. Paul is well if shabbily dressed. Surely that is, or used to be, a Harris tweed jacket with leather patches at the elbows in best university style? He tells me later that he studied at the free university of Western Australia but left without a degree. It worries me that she has known him for only three weeks, and that she looks so pale and that she has ladders in her stockings; and I hope that if ever I get married, it will be in a white dress with a lot of people there, and in a church, which would somehow make it seem more permanent.

It worries me too that Paul seems too old for her, and has needed to get, well, not drunk, but a bit . . . tanked up? tiddly? inebriated? to get him through this ordeal. He is not *drunk* as I know it — and I have known all sorts of drunks in my time: argumentative drunks, foul-mouthed drunks, violent drunks, spewy drunks, giggly and glassy-eyed drunks, maudlin drunks, and totally out-of-it drunks.

Paul is none of these. His speech is ever-so-slightly slurred, and he exudes a kind of exaggerated old-world courtesy which I understand is the result of his English public school background. It is certainly an improvement, as drunkenness goes.

For me, it all adds up to just one more dangerous secret for me to keep my mouth shut about. There is also an up-side for me. Jennie is five years older than me and at twenty-five had begun to seem in danger of being left on the shelf. If she couldn't make it, what hope would I have? So, as she has made it, perhaps even I . . . ?

Paul seems to like me, and I like him best of all the boyfriends. He gives up his room and moves in with Jennie, and soon he is spending as much time at our place as he is at Jennie's. Daddy likes him too, and before Mother dies they go out on binges together, and come home not drunk or disgusting or violent, just merry.

One night they bring a spatchcock home, and it parades squawking from bedpost to bedpost on the end of Mother's bed where she lies sick, to the accompaniment of a string of hilarious anecdotes from Daddy and Paul as to how they came by it. They have been having a very good time indeed and they set us all laughing, even Mother. Jennie is not laughing.

Some days before the exams for the final year of my arts degree, Mother persuades Daddy (or was it the other way round? — the edges have become increasingly blurred) to drive over to St Kilda and persuade Jennie to come home *where she belongs*. When I hear this, I am stricken with a sudden illness and have to fall into bed with the blankets pulled up and my eyes tightly shut. But I hear the car come back, and almost before the engine has died, before Mother can get out of the car, Daddy is in my room, looming over me, larger than ten men, his eyes blazing.

'You knew!' he hisses. 'You knew!'

'No! No!' I shriek, without even waiting to be told what it is I am supposed to know. But he is so close that he is looking right into my eyes, and whatever he sees there stops him in his tracks, and he backs out of the room without another word.

I do not understand. I am just relieved to be still alive.

One night a few weeks later, and Mother has died by now, when Daddy and I are in the back seat of Paul's car, I hear Paul, still or again inebriated, saying lovingly to Jennie: 'We got married, Jennie and I! It's a month today! And Emma was the witness. Good old Emma was —'

Jennie pokes him in the ribs and shuts him up; Daddy and I stare straight ahead without moving a muscle, and we all go off to play Solo with some friends of Paul's.

So it seems it is to be business as usual.

Mother has been ill for years. As well as her asthma, she has a hysterectomy, after which we are told that she is very ill and may not recover. She does, and is home again very soon, cheerful and talkative and apparently all right. She has trouble with her back, and Daddy, uncomplaining, drives her to the hospital three days a week for diathermy treatment. She has her appendix out, and again we are warned that she is at death's door, and again she comes home laughing about her narrow escape.

Hospital visiting has become part of my routine.

A few days before my final exams, after an ordinary visit to the asthma clinic she is admitted to the hospital because her heart is playing up. Why aren't we prepared, after all those scares? Because she always bounces back so quickly, and because it is unthinkable that she should die before me. She has been there from the beginning, so *of course* she will be there till the end! An old saying of Daddy's comes into my mind: 'You couldn't kill her with an axe!'; but I think it was me he was talking about.

I go into the hospital to visit her for the last time, though I don't know that, and she is cheerful and laughing and skiting about her kids: 'My son is in the army, one of the first to join, and this is my daughter, she's at university.'

I am snotty, and angry with her for being glad about Jock being in the army, and being proud of me because I am a university student, instead of just being proud of *us*, and I am in a hurry to get home and do some work before tea. Jennie and Paul and Jock and Daddy are all going out to a party, so I will have a whole evening to go over the notes on Aristotle's

Poetics that I carefully compiled back in first term. Realising it will take all my concentration to remember what it was all about, I have left the whole weekend to go over them for the exam on Monday.

The two younger children are in bed asleep and I am deep into it when there's a knock at the door. Who could it be? We have no visitors these days, and it is too late for bill-collectors.

A policeman. 'Does Mr Wiltshire live here?'

I wonder what he has done, but the policeman's next words are about Mother.

'I've had a ring from the Alfred Hospital about your mother. You should go in and see her. She's had a bad turn.'

Even then I am not dismayed.

'I was in to see her about six and she was fine.'

'You'd better ring the hospital,' he says and goes away.

The nurse I get onto when I ring passes me onto a sister, who wants to know is my father there and who I am, and I am beginning to feel a little strange by now.

'I'm her daughter,' I say, and *suddenly I am not even quite sure that this is true.*

'Have you someone with you?' And when I say I have (the two younger children are in bed asleep), she says: 'I'm afraid your mother has died. She had a heart attack and we weren't able to save her.'

I let the receiver dangle from the hook and break out into loud crying, and my little sister wakes and comes running, and I tell her, and we cry together and are frightened as well. I sit up nearly all night until they come home. It is 3 a.m. and they are all a bit drunk, and someone smells of spew. I tell Jennie, and she tells Daddy. I can't, for some reason.

Part of me refuses to believe that she is dead. Mistakes have been made! What if they were to bury her alive?

I have to see it for myself. So on Monday morning, before I go to the exam, I go to the mortuary parlour in South Yarra to view the body. She probably has not yet been made ready for viewing, because her mouth is slackly open in a kind of grimace which I see as cruel. I am appalled, and clutch the mortuary attendant and sob for a moment, till he panics in case he has produced the wrong body for me to view. Then I come to my senses.

I go off and do what I have been doing for so long: I push it all away. I go to university and sit for the exams, trying to remember what Aristotle said two thousand years ago on the subject of fear and pity in tragedy.

The principal of Janet Clarke Hall, where I am supposed to be having my usual end of term luncheon, has been alerted, and she meets me at the door of Wilson Hall. In her kindness, she has dealt with the supervisor and arranged for me to take in a thermos and sandwiches she has brought, in case I need nourishment during the exam.

Callous, heartless wretch that I feel I am, I get down to work so successfully that towards the end, as I concentrate hard on my writing, I kick over the thermos into the cup and saucer, making a loud clatter so alien in those still and silent surroundings that every head in Wilson Hall jerks up and stares, and I have to control an urge to break out into one of my bouts of unsuitable laughter, which I am beginning to understand is often only a short step from crying. Instead, I put my head down and go on writing.

I get my degree with second class honours.

THE REAL WORLD

THE YEAR after Mother died was the worst year of my life.

In less than three months, Grandmother has died too.

Although I am miles away, I somehow see her death as clearly as if I were in the room in the little house in Sandringham; the only place where I felt welcome as a child.

Daddy is wearing his old motorbike goggles and a cap and he has his scarf pulled up over his chin. He takes the big old key from under the mat where it always sits and lets himself in. For a minute he stands inside the door and listens to Auntie Doll and her sister, the caretaking aunt, talking and laughing in the dining room at the end of the long passage. Then he slips into the bedroom and puts a pillow over Grandmother's face; she struggles briefly and it is over. He takes a wad of notes out of her handbag beside the bed, stuffs it in his pocket and is gone.

I see all this as clearly as if I were there.

Somehow I no longer doubt that what I have seen is true, and I push it all away, but this one is the worst of all. She was his mother. She was ninety-two years old.

And soon there was a third death.

Auntie Doll moved in with her son Clem and his wife and child, and I saw her only once after that. Clem came one day and sat on the veranda in the sun with Daddy and me and told us that Auntie too had died.

'Because she had not seen a doctor for over six months before her death,' he told us, 'there has to be an autopsy.'

The thought of anyone cutting up that poor emaciated body to find the cause of death seemed to me to be grotesque. And I wondered how Daddy felt about the death of his sister, the only member of his family who had kept up any contact with him. But he and Clem sat in the sun for a while and chatted about the football and Clem's job and the weather and would there be a war. If either felt any grief, neither expressed it. No-one cried.

So now Grandmother and Auntie, as well as Mother, were out of my life, and I felt a great unease coming over me, some terrible mix of fear and desolation and anxiety, and I knew I had to go. My urgent need to please him had given way to an even more urgent need to get away.

I had by now finished my degree, and the ten shillings a week from the teachers at school had finished too, so again I was dependent on Daddy. He was now selling radios for a living, and had bought himself a brand new American car, after borrowing from me the ten pounds which I had carefully set aside to pay my graduation fee. And though I could not refuse, and indeed part of me saw it as only fair, when the car was repossessed three months later, the stupid futility of it got to me and I could not forgive him. I felt he had robbed me of my degree.

I missed the ten shillings a week I had been getting from the teachers, and the feeling of independence that it gave me, and more than that I missed the feeling that someone outside the family knew I existed and would ask questions if I were missing. Meanwhile, I was dependent on Daddy for my food and lodging. I was in need of a vacation job to get me through the Diploma of Education year.

Daddy suggested I try selling radios with him.

'Mind you, having a degree won't help you in this game. The only bloke who ever worked with me who'd been to university was a nice enough bloke but absolutely hopeless as a salesman and I had to sack him,' he told me by way of encouragement. But he provided me with a sales spiel, and gave me a piece of good advice.

'Make sure you get a demo in the first house you go into,' he told me. 'It will set you up and you'll never look back.'

All I had to do was to get a 'demo' — persuade the householders who lived on the back roads around Springvale and Templestowe, which the electricity had not yet reached, to allow Daddy to install a wireless so they could see if they liked it. The wirelesses really were wirelesses, because they did not need to be connected to the electricity, but were powered by big square batteries like car batteries, so in these days in such areas they were a godsend. The actual selling would be done by Daddy.

I was an ardent radio fan myself, and my enthusiasm for the music and the serial and the news probably made me a good salesman.

The woman in the first house I went into was very discouraging.

'He'd love a wireless, and so would I, and he's got plenty of money, but he's just too mean to spend it. You'll be wasting your time. All right,' she said, when I persisted, 'he's down the paddock mending the tank.'

So down the paddock I went and tried to talk to him, in what must surely have been one of the most difficult selling situations ever. He kept hammering away at his tank while I kept hammering away at my sales pitch, determined to get a demo at the first house.

Finally he sent me back to the house while he put away his tools, and I went and talked to his wife, who was delighted that I was still afloat. It never occurred to either of us that she had any right to have an input into this decision. We amused ourselves watching the antics of a tiny kitten which had just discovered rain, hitting at a drop as it came down and turning almost somersaults to get to the next one. At last sourpuss came back (I was beginning to suspect he was not as sour underneath as he pretended to be) and he made an appointment for Daddy to bring a set for him to listen to. He eventually bought one, but I was told never to persevere with such a difficult customer again. He had made Daddy come back again and again, and forced him to lower the price so much that there was no profit in it.

On that first day I got five demos and was over the moon with delight. At last I had been successful at something Daddy thought worth doing!

That successful day was a beginning and an end for me. He began to use all his charm, all his powers of persuasion, to make me give up the idea of doing a Diploma of Education and concentrate instead on making a living selling radios with him.

'You'll make a lot more at it than you ever will going teaching,' he said. 'And we need you here at home to look after us.'

I knew it was selfish of me, but I didn't even hesitate. I had seen what happened when you worked for a relation, and I knew I had to get away. Perhaps Jennie's experience of working in Uncle George's factory, when she was paid twenty-five shillings a week for her office job and had to pay twenty of it back to Daddy as board, was too recent.

And though he was furious, and I felt selfish and ungrateful, he couldn't move me. There was no fight. When he drove me to the outskirts now, he left me there, and I sat under a tree till he picked me up, a past master at the art of passive resistance. I never got another demo. He knew that what I wanted most was to get away and that I would do it somehow, as Jennie and Jock had done, whatever he did or said. And it was Grandmother and the graduation money that gave me the strength to resist.

Everything changed.

Jennie and Paul had moved out to the other side of town; Jock had gone overseas with the army.

Daddy took up with a woman called Gladys, recently divorced from her husband Frank. Frank had been a friend of my father's for years. He usually had the butt of a moist skinny home-rolled cigarette hanging limply from his lower lip, and talked somehow through it. I had always liked him because though he drank, he never got drunk, and was always nice to me. He told Daddy that he wanted to marry me.

'You can have her for fifty quid,' said Daddy. 'After all the money I've spent on her education, I can't let her go for nothing.'

I was enraged.

'He's old!' I said to myself. 'He's nearly as old as Daddy!'

When he told Daddy that I didn't want to marry him, Daddy was enraged too.

'Don't ask her what she wants!' he roared. 'Tell her what *you* want!'

But Frank was too decent, or perhaps just too limp. He faded and Gladys moved in. Within nine months of Mother's death, they were married.

We had known her for years, and found her mildly interesting as an A-grade tennis player and the owner of a wonderful Samoyed dog which did tricks. Gladys would put a piece of meat on the floor, wag a stern finger at the dog and say: 'It's mortgaged!' The dog would wag its tail and watch and wait until the release came: 'Paid for!' and it would wolf it down. The dog seemed to understand and enjoy the game as much as Gladys and Frank.

When they divorced, Frank somehow got custody of the dog and Gladys was desolate. When she started appearing again with Daddy, she was a new Gladys, coy and kittenish and talking baby talk to him. I found it disgusting, but he was purring. They were married, and she moved in.

She started complaining to me almost at once. 'I didn't want to get married till we had saved some money,' she whined, 'but he made me.'

I gave her no sympathy.

'You're a grown woman,' I said to her. 'It's no use blaming him. You have to make your own decisions.'

But secretly I was sorry for her landing in a hotbed of Wiltshires and enormously grateful to her for easing the guilt I felt at the prospect of leaving the two smaller children — who had somehow always seemed to belong to a different family from the one Jock and Jennie and I had grown up into — at home with Daddy. The job was now hers, and was no doubt much harder than looking after the Samoyed.

Jennie was enraged at Gladys's takeover. I think she may have been jealous, and even though I did not want to stay home, I would have liked to be the centre of attention myself for a little while.

In every way I found Gladys hard to believe. She told me she'd never read a book in her life, and she needed help to write out the shopping list. Was this her attraction? Was it true that intelligent men prefer women with looks but no brains? If so, I was done for, already tarred with the brush of being dux of two schools and now irrevocably a bluestocking with an honours degree. Where was I to find a minor Einstein beside whom I would seem a bear of very little brain? I soothed myself with the realisation that the family all still regarded me as pretty stupid, and wondered if I might have to go through life doing what I had always done at home, remembering nothing and knowing nothing, or at least accepting my role as the stupid one.

Even after explaining her attraction in this way, I found it hard to believe that Daddy had married her. She was the antithesis of everything that Daddy had taught me about a man's requirements in a wife.

First, she was over forty, and 'a man of forty is just entering the prime of life, but a woman of forty is over the hill.'

She was fat. And to me in fifth form, when I put on a bit of weight: 'You'll have to get that weight off, Emma, or no man's ever going to look at you.'

She had been divorced and was therefore 'another man's leavings', 'damaged goods', another reason for disqualification.

The coy and kittenish one disappeared as soon as they were married, and so did the purring one, and ructions began almost immediately, but they were very small potatoes compared with my then very hazy and quickly pushed away recollections of the ructions of my early childhood.

Daddy's attempts to make Gladys toe the line began almost immediately, but were frustrated by her skill and speed in nipping into next door to tell the neighbours on him — a new experience for him.

Once there was a blow-up during Sunday dinner, and he let out a mighty bull-roar and hurled his roast dinner at her. The plate missed and hit the wall. It didn't break, but the meat and several baked potatoes, gravy, peas and pumpkin, slid gracefully and colourfully down the wall. I managed not to laugh. I was convinced that if the plate had broken, the tension would have broken too. Instead, he jumped up more enraged than ever and rushed at her, and, ever the peacemaker, I leapt on his back with my arm round his throat till he calmed down. Gladys was already out the door. Daddy and I avoided each other's eyes for a few days, and life went on.

In that last year at university, I missed Mother, who though she sometimes drank too much and was generally sick and often cantankerous, could sometimes be relied upon to come through as mediator between Daddy and his children. I hated being alone in the house with him for some reason, and once I had refused to give up my course, relations between us were very strained. Until Gladys moved in, he still needed me to do the housework and look after the younger children, Georgia and Brian, and I still needed him to provide me with food and a bed. Neither of us liked it. I felt totally inadequate for the job I had to do.

Brian came out with an infection of impetigo all round his mouth. The chemist told me how to wash the sores off with hot salted water night and morning, and said he needed lots of vegetables, which I often had no money to provide. Georgia broke her arm at school. Daddy was not around and I took her to the doctor to get it set, but I was afraid of being blasted for taking too much on myself when the bill came in, and guilty too about running up a bill which my father wouldn't pay.

Before Gladys surfaced, he had taken to staying away and sleeping somewhere else on several nights, and I would be left with no money for food or fares, and when he came home I would make a scene, but I felt like a nagging wife and that if I couldn't manage it must be because of my own inadequacy. The belief that everything was my fault had been too well dinned in.

My troubles at home now began to spill over to university. In the school of education, I was earning a reputation for being unreliable. Sometimes I did not have the money for the fare to get me to some out-of-town school where I was supposed to watch a good teacher give a demonstration lesson, or to give one myself in front of an experienced teacher or a university lecturer. If I couldn't get there, I generally rang up to say I was sick, or gave some other weak excuse, but after the phone was cut off sometimes I didn't even have the money for a phone call and I just didn't turn up.

Standing up in front of a class with a lecturer or experienced teacher watching was an ordeal, probably not helped by the fact that I had spent the last three years sitting reading books and talking in the cafeteria, and the only demands made on me were a breeze — that I assimilate and digest enough to pass the exams. I could write my answers and never have to look at what I had written again. This was different. I had to talk! I had stand up and talk to and in front of strangers!

On bad days I was disorganised and dithery; a senior English teacher and a central school headmaster both blasted me right out of the water for being too superficial and for insufficient preparation. It never occurred to me to blame anything other than my own stupidity. It never occurred to me that some of those other, well-brought-up girls were nearly as dopey in this new situation as I was, or that they were suffering similar trials at the hands of such competent but unhelpful people.

I concentrated on surviving the year. I think I only survived because other lecturers praised my teaching. One said I had an attractive personality. Another, making a few suggestions as to how the lesson might have been improved, said to me: 'You laughed a lot with the children, and that made the lesson a pleasure for them and for me watching it.'

To actually be praised — and for laughing!

Such praise was balm to my soul, and gave me the strength to go on.

I scraped through by the skin of my teeth.

After I finished university, I got a job for six weeks in a munitions factory and worked thirteen days a fortnight with overtime to get enough money to buy myself a few clothes and a pair of shoes, to save enough for my fare to the country town where I had been appointed, and to pay my board for two weeks.

And I left home.

To leave home seemed to me both the best and the worst thing I could ever do.

I would be escaping from a place where I had always felt I had no right to be, and where I had been given responsibility for two children whose mother had died suddenly, and whose father was often not there. It was a role I did not want and could not fill.

When I left home on that Saturday morning, Georgia and Brian were off to the movies, and Daddy and Gladys were off to the races at Flemington and dropped me at Spencer Street station, leaving me to carry my own case to the train. This was not a problem — my worldly goods only half filled it.

There were no tearful farewells, no hugs and kisses. This was not the family style. Daddy made no verbal comment about my departure, but his unspoken ones came across to me loud and clear: 'You won't know what's hit you when you're out in the real world! If you go, don't come back!'

So part of me was full of guilt at leaving the children and full of grief that I was unable to bridge any of the gaps and express even part of the love, hate, fear that I was feeling; but part of me was full of triumph and elation.

I was leaving home for the real world!

CAREER GIRL

ARMED WITH enough money for two weeks' board, a suitcase half full of clothes and minimal teaching skills, I got off the train at Colac and went looking for a place to board.

Jock had once roared at me: 'Don't come the bloody Pollyanna around here, always looking on the bright side!' I didn't feel much like Pollyanna when I settled in to Mrs O'Leary's boarding house.

Panic set in. What if, as they said, I couldn't last five minutes on my own? What if I got the sack, as I had once after one night at a milk bar, because I was too slow? It was ninety miles to Melbourne, and I didn't have the fare home, even assuming I would be taken in when I got there.

But if I had been slow in the milk bar, I was quick off the mark in landing the local electrician, who also boarded at Mrs O'Leary's, as a boyfriend on my second night away. That is, for almost a year we went to the pictures twice a week, once a week he bought me chocolates, and once a week I went to his place, where his mother, approving, gave us tea and then left us to discover the joys and terrors of the grope on the couch. Ian was older than I was and very intent on progressing past the grope stage, but had very little idea as to how to bring that about. While half of me wanted to have exciting affairs like Jennie, mostly I was intent on getting married and having a baby, in that order. I was under bond to the Education Department for three and a half years after graduation because they had paid my fees for the diploma year, so marriage seemed out of the question, though later I learnt of other girls with more gumption who'd blithely disregarded the ban and got married or pregnant, a still greater sin, and escaped without paying the bond.

A need at this stage even more important to me than marriage was for some life of my own, some freedom, some experience. I felt I had left the nest without learning to flap my wings. And I wanted money! I not only wanted money, I needed it.

The untold wealth which my pay-check had seemed to promise did not eventuate. I started immediately paying back the money I had borrowed from the teachers, and never missed a payment till it was paid. Because I had not paid the fee to graduate, I was designated 'B.A. Qualified' and paid less than the salary for a graduate, as well as being paid, as a woman, at a considerably lower rate than the men. I also had to pay superannuation, which I resented because I simply could not visualise myself as living long enough to collect it, and anyway, I was going to get married, wasn't I? And then I wouldn't need superannuation. The superannuation could not be collected until you were sixty-five, unless you were leaving to marry, in which case you would be given eighty-five per cent of it back. Against Daddy's advice, I paid five shillings a week for an insurance policy. I knew I'd do better to put it in the bank at compound interest, but I also knew I wouldn't put it in the bank, I'd spend it. The superannuation would eventually pay for my wedding breakfast, and the insurance policy, when it matured, would buy us a block of land by the seaside, where I and my husband and our three children would spend all our school holidays for years.

But the imagined wealth of being employed soon became quite difficult to manage on. I was still hard up, but oh! the blissful feeling of independence, of not being dependent on Daddy's charity, as I paid my weekly board and had a little left over for myself! Of buying myself some clothes — new shoes, a skirt, a jumper, a wonderful royal blue coat — clothes that fitted, that I chose, that hadn't belonged to someone else before I got them! Of being away from home at last!

And oh! the bliss of having a boyfriend, who seemed to think I was lovely, and who I didn't have to take home to be charmed away by Daddy!

The bliss of having no-one to criticise, or forbid, or give orders, or to be dependent on! There was a phrase used by people in those circles where girls made their debut — they 'came out'. I think I had been coming out of those early dark ages ever since I went to university, and leaving to go to Colac was an important step forward.

More enterprising staff boarded at the pub, but my memories of lots of red-faced boozy men from when, as a small girl, I went to the pub at Carnegie to buy Abbotsford Invalid Stout for my mother put me off that. Instead I boarded with three other women at the establishment of Miss Cahill, an 'old maid'. She had an enormous bosom, and told me with great good humour that someone had dared her to see if she could rest a tray on it. She could! One of the other boarders was a secretary at the butter factory. I spent some energy trying to avoid her, and she spent some energy trying to get me into a corner to tell me how awful Miss Cahill was. I was fascinated to realise that she had a five o'clock shadow and needed to shave every day, but naïve as I was, I drew no conclusions. Another boarder was a recent euphoric convert to Catholicism, who went to confession six times a week during Lent. Conditioned as I was, I could see no evidence of significant sin in her and found it hard to understand that it would take a whole week to clean it up. She explained that you could sin in word, thought or deed, a pretty scary thought. The third was the senior mistress at the high school, who assisted me with any difficulties I had at school and who warned me obliquely about the sad waste of another young protégé of hers who had taken up with a young man in the town and married him and had children, thus destroying for ever her chance of a career.

When a new senior mistress with a passion for golf was appointed, she took me and others out to the golf club every day after school and gave us lessons. She said I showed promise and gave me her old set of clubs when she bought a new lot. I will never forget the exhilaration of those afternoons in the fresh chill air on the hill at the golf club, and the marvellous sound the golf ball made when you hit it just right and it landed just where you wanted it to land.

Miss Cahill fed us like lords on the produce of her farm, and blew a breath of fresh air over me one day when I confided to her that I was known as the placid one in my family. It was the family myth, and till then I suppose I had believed it. Miss Cahill literally laughed till she cried. As she wiped the tears away, she gasped: 'Well, I'd like to see the rest of them!'

She never gave me any advice, and so it was on her shoulder that I cried when the telegram came reporting Jock MISSING, BELIEVED PRISONER OF WAR. I had cried when he left, convinced that I would never see him again, and the telegram seemed like a confirmation of my fears.

Miss Cahill didn't say much other than 'Oh dear!' and 'There, there!', but she put her arms around me and let me cry it out. No-one will ever convince me that being an old maid means there's something wrong with you!

I still went home for weekends sometimes, partly to check that Georgia and Brian were all right, partly from homesickness, and partly from a need to go back

for something of my own that I had lost there —
perhaps my heart, or my head even — I didn't know. I
always took presents, things I knew were needed: an
enamel teapot, some rump steak — the teapot was too
big, the rump steak tough. I bought Brian a new suit, a
quilt and pillow cases for Georgia, and I paid Brian's
dentist's bill. It eased my guilt about having stayed at
school for so long.

Daddy then asked me for fifty pounds, a massive sum
to me, to pay a speeding fine. I didn't mind contributing
for necessities, but a speeding fine! Something he could
have avoided! So though I gave him the money and said
nothing, underneath I dared to be angry. In the night I
had one of my 'seeings', the first and last for many years.
I saw him coming home in the car from Preston at two
o'clock in the morning when he was stopped by the
police. They gave him a ticket for speeding — they very
perfunctory, he very apologetic, deferential.

As he drove away, he changed. I saw him sweating
and shaking with fear.

'If they'd looked in the boot!' was all he said.

I did not want to know what was in the boot.

I paid the fifty pounds but I was angry and afraid,
as though I were an accessory after the fact of
whatever it was. He did not ask me for money again.

I went home one weekend when Georgia was there.
We talked and laughed in bed till long after midnight,
till Daddy roared: 'Shut up the pair of you! If you
don't shut up, I'll come in and shut you up, and I don't
care how old you are!'

And the old fear, buried deep as it was, surfaced again and I became once more a frightened child.

In Colac, Ian's and my affair was grinding almost to a halt, and he joined the airforce and was gone. After he left, you could have shot a cannon at any time of night or day down Main Street without hitting a man under sixty, and Wednesdays and Saturdays were empty.

And almost immediately, as if in answer to my unexpressed wish, I was whisked away by the Education department to teach at Bairnsdale, where I was told there were three thousand young aircrew doing an operational training course before they went into action.

When I got off the train after my long trip, I was met by a young teacher from the high school called Maeve, who had been sent to bring me to be interviewed by the headmaster. I did think it might have waited till morning, but he had his reasons.

The local newspaper had been running a campaign criticising the high school for poor results in the external examinations and for the lack of qualified teachers, especially English teachers, on the staff. Almost before the head and I had finished exchanging names and warily inspecting each other, the phone rang.

The head handed the phone to me.

'It's for you,' he said. 'It's the editor of the local paper. He wants to know what your qualifications are.'

It was nice to be able to trot out my honours degree with a major in English, to the sound of an audible sigh of relief from the head and clucks of interest from the editor. Next morning one of my mother's worst fears was realised: I was written up in the local paper. My honours degree made the front page and was claimed as a triumph by the newspaper as a result of its campaign. I didn't care who got the credit — it felt like a welcome.

Maeve and I became friends, and after a couple of weeks in an appalling boarding house, we moved into a tiny furnished flat together. If boarding at Miss Cahill's had seemed wonderful after home, living in the flat was heaven. We cooked our own sketchy meals when we felt like it. Maeve swears that the only sweet I knew how to cook was banana custard made with Foster Clark's custard powder, and her cooking was not much better. Once, we set fire to the enormous upstairs chimney through burning newspaper in it to keep warm, and the fire brigade had to come and put it out. Maeve was also in disgrace when, after a trip along the river with an airman in a boat with an oily bottom, she left oily footmarks on the bath we shared with the owner and the other tenants. She was a Catholic and never missed mass, even when we went to Lakes Entrance, where she had to walk two miles to church. I was impressed by such devotion. Unlike my fellow boarder at Colac, she was, however, not euphoric. When she came home, I was often still in bed with a book and it made her furious.

'If you're in heaven when I get there, Emma Wiltshire,' she stormed, 'there's going to be some explaining to do!'

The three thousand young aircrew, very attractive in their uniforms — the 'blue orchids', as the envious army boys in their shoddy and ugly clothes called them — were well-educated and out to enjoy life as much as they could, while they could. One bright-eyed boy, an air-gunner, told me simply that the life of an air-gunner in combat was two and a half minutes. He was facing the sort of reality I could not bear to face. Those boys were not prevented by the considerable demands of their course and the uncertainties of their futures from giving the girls of Bairnsdale a good time. We went to dances two or three times a week, and danced with airmen and local farmers and the senior boys from school. A few of the airmen sensed a tension in my dancing and urged me to 'let myself go', but I had unconsciously fought against doing that since the last time I had opened the garage doors for Daddy, when, after a blow on the head, I had listened to my own small voice and started to tell the truth of who killed who, and the whole family had followed Daddy's lead and rushed at me, so that I felt I could never count on any of them again.

One girl I admired at the dances had no such inhibitions. She was Topsy, the first jitterbug I had ever seen. She jitterbugged with a skill and timing and athleticism that I have never seen since. She wore the sort of suitable clothes that made it seem immaterial that you could often see her matching pants right up to her waist, which in those days should have been shocking but wasn't. It didn't seem to be a sexual display at all. The airmen stood in a queue of nine or ten waiting for the privilege of trying out their skills with her. Beside her I felt like the wooden doll Uncle Don had made for me.

'Why can't you be more like other girls?' my mother had groaned, but I don't think she meant Topsy.

We went sometimes to dances in halls in outlying districts, where in those days of rationing, the farmers' wives made us sponges of gossamer lightness with passionfruit icing and filled with thick wonderful cream, and tall cheese or sultana scones with wonderful rationed butter melting into them and around them.

Life became a party, a party to which I was invited.

We went to movies, and on ferry trips down the Mitchell to Lakes Entrance, where we stayed in borrowed houses. We played some terrible tennis and some worse golf and we swam, though my swimming always had an element of pure terror in it and was always more puff and gasp than progression in the water. We made ourselves some sometimes terrible clothes.

Perhaps the best thing was having a friend who seemed to accept me without much friction. And not only a friend, but friends, for the staff at school were very young and friendly, and some of the airmen were friendly, and asked nothing more: some because they were married and others, like the boys at Blackwood, who just liked having girls around.

After a time, Maeve had an affair with an airman and I with a local teacher. I will always remember him as the one who made me feel that, contrary to my expectations, sex could be pleasurable and that Hemingway's description of sex as 'the little death' was perhaps only a metaphor. And yet . . . and yet . . .

Feeling wickedly extravagant, Maeve and I went at vacation time to Tasmania on what seemed an intrepid trip in a little aeroplane — a D.C. 4? — with seats arranged around both sides like an old-fashioned bus. There I discovered the joys of crayfish at two shillings a plate, fresh out of an incredibly blue and clean and beautiful Derwent river, washed down with draughts of apple cider. I had never tasted cider before but soon acquired the taste for it, and fortunately, given oaths and Methodism, I was so naïve that I didn't learn it was alcoholic till later. I'm sure it contributed a lot to the pleasure of our trip.

I took two lobsters home to Daddy over the protests of the taxi driver who was driving us to the airport: 'They won't let you take those things on a plane, lady! They stink!'

'I'll wrap them in a lot of paper,' I said. 'They won't know what I've got!'

'They'll know they ain't violets!' he said.

They were not well received (I don't eat crayfish, and don't come the lady bountiful with me, miss!), and as I handed them over I felt his eyes going over me, inch by inch, in my clinging grey woollen dress with the vieux rose suede collar and belt, happy and well and full of vitality after my wonderful holiday. All he said was: 'There's nothing like sex to make the world go round, is there, Em?' And he smiled. And I knew he knew that I had grown up. And for the first time for years, I listened to and heard and understood what I had been blocking out for years, his other voice: 'I'd like to have her in my bed again!'

And the old world that I thought I had escaped from moved in.

There was a letter from Jock in Switzerland, telling me that he was safe and well and as the war in Europe was now over he would soon be home. With him would be coming a beautiful French girl called Manette.

After the letter from Jock there was a letter from the Education department. I was transferred from Bairnsdale to a school in East Camberwell. Maeve was transferred to Warrnambool.

The good times were over.

I moved back into the family home, but now I was under few illusions about how welcome I was. Gladys was glad of my intervention when she was threatened with physical violence, but was very much the boss in the domestic sphere, though none of her new charges was as amenable as the Samoyed had been, and the situation must have been almost as difficult for her as it was for me.

Maeve's affair with her airman and mine with my teacher ended.

I was loath to take a boy home. My teacher had spoken of a long-standing arrangement with a girl in Melbourne, who he was half-expected to marry, and I felt I couldn't compete. The last reason seemed shameful and ridiculous: that I suddenly felt I needed a very much bigger and stronger man, who could protect me if I needed it. From what I still was not sure.

The school I was appointed to was a girls' school, and academically the best I had yet taught in, though Bairnsdale will always have first place in my heart for the pupils and the staff and the dancing and the friendships I enjoyed there, as well as for the beauty of the place itself. At Camberwell the classes were graded as they had been at MacRobertson High. I taught the brightest classes and also the least academic, and I had to set an examination paper for pupils at both ends of the scale to answer. Form 3A, having hung on my every word during classes, wrote pages of foolscap in answer to each question, and my marking was as tough as Miss Lehman's had been with me. Forms 3EF often wrote only a line or two, reducing the issue to its ultimate simplicity, but I sneakily gave them a mark if their one-liners showed they had understood the question and had some clue about what the answer should be. I prayed I wouldn't get found out.

I got on well with the staff, knew I was teaching well and was enjoying it, but I knew too that I had to get away from home as soon as possible.

I applied for the first position that was advertised — at Bendigo High School — and I didn't get it. It was given instead to a young man whose qualifications and experience were not as good as mine, and who was lower on the department's seniority roll.

As I sat grizzling at lunchtime in the staffroom about the unfairness of it all, the senior mistress, Miss Gilford, broke in on our conversation.

'Why don't you stop moaning and do something about it?' she said tersely.

'Who? Me? What could I possibly do?'

And she told me.

Miss Gilford was the second in command at the school but we all knew that she was the one who really ran it. The headmistress sometimes rushed around roaring and flapping till Miss G. found out what was wrong, soothed the head and fixed the problem. Apart from those small crises, the school seemed to run itself. Other staff members had whispered to me that Miss G. was a lesbian, possibly for no other reason than that she lived with another woman. I was no more enlightened about lesbians than the rest of the staff — it was the first time I had heard the word, except in Jock's limerick about the 'Young man from Khartoum

> *Who took a lesbian up to his room,*
> *And as he turned off the light*
> *He said, "Let's get this right —*
> *Who does what, and with which, and to whom?"'*

I could only imagine what the answers were.

If Miss G. was a lesbian, she certainly didn't fancy me, but in a most capable and professional way she told me exactly what to do about the job in Bendigo.

'Appeal!' she said.

And she took time from her many responsibilities to direct me into getting the official form and filling it in and writing the appeal; more importantly, she made it seem that insisting on my rights was not unutterably selfish but simply right and fair, and that I was a fool if I didn't.

With her support, I stood up well in the interview with the seven secondary inspectors (six of them men) on the appeals board, and though they were fishing to know why I was anxious to leave Melbourne when other people were clamouring to stay there, I managed to handle that without giving too much away and I got the job.

Once again freedom was in sight.

JOCK

SOME MEMORIES are not my memories at all. They are Jock's memories mixed up with my own, old ones and new ones jumbled up almost as incoherently as my own will be when I first begin to let myself remember.

So what are Jock's memories doing in the middle of my memoir?

They are here because Jock has always been part of my life, and because he is part of the pleasure and awfulness of this part of my life.

There was the pleasure of the Camberwell school, with an efficient staff and a new senior mistress, a woman of very different calibre from any woman I had yet met. She ran things. She didn't let me sit and grizzle when there was something I could do to mend the situation. She showed me what to do.

I began to realise that in this congenial atmosphere I was teaching well and that my pupils, both academic and non-academic, were enjoying my lessons and getting a lot out of them. My confidence in my own powers was growing.

The awful side of this picture was the return to the family home.

This time I was not as emotionally dependent as I used to be. I had accepted that I was not welcome, and perhaps because I had not been eaten alive in the big world, I knew that I would survive.

I had accepted that Mother and Daddy and Jock and Jennie were all part of the rush at me after the bang on the head by the garage doors, and deep down I knew that Daddy was too powerful for any of the others to support me against him.

Jock's particular importance dates from an even earlier time, when I was forbidden to talk to the others and they were forbidden to talk to me, until finally Daddy had relented.

'She'll go crazy if she doesn't have someone to talk to, and be even more trouble. Let her talk to Jock. He can keep her in order!'

So Jock was enormously important as the only one I could talk to. (He would save me from going crazy?) And some part of me also saw him as wonderful, my link with the outside world.

But another part of me resented his assumption that he was always right, that he was the one who gave the orders and my role was to obey.

Before I make my escape to my new appointment to Bendigo he tells some of his memories to me, in my role of good listener who says little, after he comes back from the war, when I too am a reluctant inmate of the family home once more, sleeping on a bed in the sitting room, with my clothes hanging on hangers from the mantelpiece. He is much more talkative and articulate than he was when we were children. He has been away from the family for five and a half years, first as a signalman in the infantry in England and North Africa, then as a prisoner of war in Italy, and finally as an internee in Switzerland. He tells me stories about the war that make me laugh and cry, and I look in admiration at this little brother, this man, who has been through so many adventures and so many hardships, while all I have been doing is getting a degree and having inconclusive love affairs and working as a teacher.

Of the actual war and its dangers he tells me very little. As a signaller, his job was to creep out at night, sometimes alone, sometimes under sporadic shelling, to install or repair telephone lines or alarm systems on the perimeters of the defended areas, which must have been pretty scary. But the stories he tells me are mostly light-hearted ones about the war and the prisoner-of-war camp and his internment in Switzerland.

During the siege of Tobruk, he tells me, a group of men sat around together in a circle, talking and laughing and smoking during a peaceful interlude in the hostilities. 'We lived so close,' he says, 'that nothing was hidden.'

'One of the blokes was talking his head off,' says Jock, 'and decided to have a shit at the same time. While he was busy talking, one of us took a handful of sand and hurled it over the turd. He turned round to look at what he had done,' — Jock is laughing as he remembers it — 'but there was nothing there. And he was in such a rage, as though he had been robbed of a priceless treasure, that we all rolled in the sand laughing at him.'

He tells of the appalling boredom in the prisoner-of-war camp, when they had nothing more interesting to do day after day than pick the lice out of the seams of their shirts. Once, he and a few others were detailed to go out into the rice fields and help with the harvesting. He tells of his joy at being for a few weeks out in the natural world again with women around, after the oppression of the camp.

Again his story comes down to the most basic human functions.

'There were no men in the rice fields except the P.O.W.s and a few guards,' he says, 'and when the women needed to relieve themselves they would just go over to a ditch at the side and pull up their dresses, and just do it and come back, as though it were the most natural thing in the world.'

In the world of our childhood, such functions had not been 'the most natural thing in the world'. Very early they had become a duty to be performed at a certain time in a certain place, and any lapse filled our parents with anger and disgust and threats and beatings, so such stories have a certain charm for both of us.

Other stories are not so pleasant. He tells of the fearful food shortages. Because the guards were by then just as hungry as the prisoners, when the Red Cross parcels came they would pilfer half the contents before the prisoners got them, so the war went on, even in the camp. Of how some men had cravings for particular foods and would swap anything — 'even cigarettes!' says Jock in amazement — for a can of meat or for cheese or for condensed milk.

'Before the parcels came,' Jock tells me, 'all we talked about was food. We would read books like *Lorna Doone*, where there were pages of descriptions of food, and tell of what our mothers or wives had cooked for us that we liked; and after the food parcels arrived for more than a week we would talk about nothing but sex. Then it was back to food.'

The Australians in the camp offered to teach the 'Camp Commandant', as they called him, to speak English, planning to pick up a little Italian for themselves by the way. Being Australians they taught him the language with a certain flair. One day the commandant was up on his platform, haranguing the prisoners over some crime or misdemeanor they had committed.

'You th-think I don't know anything about it!' he stuttered, red in the face with rage, 'but I t-tell you I know *fuck all*!'

It brought the house down.

The escape from the prisoner-of-war camp had been not so much an escape as an eviction. The Italian authorities by then knew that the war was lost, and saw the Germans as being as much the enemy as the allies, who were advancing from the south. They concentrated on saving their own skins and left the camp open. Some of the prisoners who left at once were machine-gunned by Germans, so there was a very uncertain situation for a while. Eventually Jock and his friend slipped out together, and because their colouring was dark, they knew a little Italian and there were only two of them, they fared better than most and eventually got on a train that went north.

There they joined up with a band of partisans, but their Italian was so poor that they could not melt into the villages as the partisans did after a raid and became a liability, so before long they were provided with boots, food and a guide, and they were escorted over a pass in the Alps to Switzerland.

The guide left them at the top of a ridge.

'You're in Switzerland already,' he told them. 'Just keep going in the same direction for a couple of days and you should come to a settlement. Good luck!'

They plodded on in sometimes blinding snowstorms in what they hoped was still the same direction until their supplies were exhausted and they could hardly shuffle along because of frost-bitten feet. They were almost ready to do what the guide had warned them against doing — lie down in the snow and go to sleep. Suddenly they heard the sound of an axe on wood.

'Best sound I ever heard in my life!' says Jock.

In a few days they were in hospital, their frost-bitten feet packed in ice (I seemed to have heard of someone being packed in ice once before) and were cared for till they recovered.

In hospital Jock met a beautiful French-speaking girl called Manette, who spoke three languages, none of them English, and who conversed with him in halting Italian, and very soon after he came out of hospital they became lovers.

After the wars at home, the wars in the desert and the prisoner-of-war camp, Switzerland, with regular food and shelter and the days spent playing serious contract bridge and tobogganing and most nights spent with Manette, must have seemed like heaven.

When the war in Europe finished and Jock was on his way home, he went back to Italy and saw starvation even worse than it had been in the prisoner-of-war camp, and what he saw sickened him.

'In a lot of little narrow streets,' he says, 'there were rows of tiny little houses, and through the uncurtained windows of one of them I saw three women lying naked on the bed — the mother and the daughter and the grandmother — and you could have had any one of them for a bar of chocolate or a can of beef.'

In the middle of his war stories, he tells me some tales about Grandfather Wiltshire, who I realise is one person about whom — and I was seven when he died so I could be expected to have some memories of him — I remember nothing except what Jennie and Jock and Mother have told me.

Jennie told me her memory after her breakdown, and she told it to me two or three times, and I could see that for her it was a pleasant one.

'He called me his little woman,' she says, 'and when Mother and I lived with Grandmother, he took me everywhere with him. And I played up on him! If he wouldn't give me a lolly or whatever it was I wanted, I'd lie down on the footpath and kick my legs up in the air and yell at the top of my voice and refuse to go on till he gave in.'

Grandfather would arrive home distraught, and tell Grandmother: 'I'm never going to take that child anywhere ever again.'

But he always did.

Mother's story is a funny one. When she lived with them while Daddy was away, she would be awakened every morning by the sound of Grandfather's slippers flop-flop-flopping along the linoleum of the long passage as he sped to the outside lavatory. 'And,' says Mother, enjoying her story, 'with very step he would fart loudly, and I would be lying in bed trying to stifle my laughter in the quilt so he wouldn't hear me.'

Jock's story about Grandfather is of staying at Grandmother's when he went there for a long stint because things were very bad at home and Mother found him unmanageable. The big treat was that Grandfather went, once a week, to the wine shop.

'We would sit down, and the woman would bring him a glass of red wine, and then a glass of lemonade and a biscuit for me. We were like two men together,' says Jock, 'and the best thing was that the woman would treat me as though I were just as important as he was. As though I *mattered*.'

Grandfather kept the money for the weekly trip to the wine shop hidden on a ledge at the top of the trellis covered with asparagus fern that screened the outside lavatory, and once when he went to get it, the money was gone.

'He went in to Grandmother,' says Jock, and his eyes are wide and his voice is full of admiration, 'and he said to her sternly: "Don't you ever touch my money again, woman!"'

I wonder why their memories of Grandfather are all happy ones while my only feeling for him is fear, both of him and of his little yapping dog that followed him everywhere and stayed at the foot of his bed when he died, and like the song about the grandfather clock that stopped short, never to go again when the old man died, Grandfather's dog also died on the next day.

My only memory of Grandfather that surfaces in the night after Jock's stories is one that would be labelled 'just her imagination', or lies, or seeing things, so I don't share it with Jock.

It is a picture memory of Grandfather saying sternly to Grandmother: 'I won't have another crying girl in the house. She should never have been allowed to see the light of day. Get rid of her before I come home on Monday!'

It is not till I am middle-aged and start putting two and two together and making often many more than four, that I connect it up with the story of the baby in the well. And later still with a memory of Daddy saying to me in one of his friendly confidential chats: 'It's a law of nature, Em. Men give the orders and women just do what they're told.'

Do men have power of life and death over women and girls?

I will read about nomadic tribes where a mother who had twins was forced to kill one, because the demands of their nomadic life made it impossible for her to look after two babies and keep up with the tribe.

Is Grandmother's response an acceptance of the social reality of her times, that if Grandfather will not support 'the crying girl' she must either get rid of it or jeopardise his protection of herself and her other four children?

I do not know.

But I know that when I married and bullied my reluctant husband into buying a house so that my children would have the stability and security that had been so lacking in my childhood, the house I had in my head was Grandmother's old Victorian house at Sandringham, with the flower garden and the may bush, where I too had been welcome.

JOCK AND I

DADDY WORKED at a munitions factory during the war, and when the war and the job finished, with his usual ingenuity, he started up something new.

He put some well-bred hens in the backyard and bought himself a huge incubator, in which he bred thousands of chickens, selling them at increasing prices according to age in weeks. A man from a chicken-sexing firm, appropriately named Mr Forecast, came periodically to sex them and, in a reversal of the human practice, it was the males that were thrown away as worthless.

Once again, because of the food left out for the chooks, there were rats running round in the ceiling.

When Jock came home from Switzerland, he was at first on leave for a few weeks. He had brought a stack of books on contract bridge home with him and was determined to convert us all. Paul had taught us to play light-hearted auction, but Paul was now gone and Jock was in charge and there was nothing light-hearted about it. He wanted me to read them all, but I half remembered learning euchre from him when I was small and having trouble with the right and left bowers, when a Jack was sometimes hearts and sometimes diamonds. I half remembered his instruction too: 'You can only play if you let me win!'

Did I say Jock was in charge? I was once again the stupid one — I couldn't or wouldn't take it all in. Daddy bid no-trumps whether he had the hand for it or not, so he could play every hand. Jock roared at me if I bid: 'Why did you fucking bid spades?', or if I didn't bid: 'Why don't you fucking bid? Bid something! Bid anything!'

I didn't want to play, but I was needed to make a four and if I didn't play it would spoil it for everyone. I sat there being uncooperative, Jock raged at us all, and I for one was glad when his leave was up and the bridge finished.

At the end of his leave, Daddy threw a party for him, and though everybody else seemed to be having a good time, I felt like a fish out of water, the one nobody wanted, the one who shouldn't be there. I was beginning to feel strange, a sort of Jekyll and Hyde, that I could be so capable and pleasant out of the house and so tense and lack-lustre inside it.

There have been other parties: parties in my childhood, parties in my teens, with beer and music and screaming and brawling, and at one of them a woman's arm is broken and the neighbours complain and the police come. Later I will remember a good party, when I am five or six, and I am allowed to stay up till nine o'clock. I am sitting on the couch beside my mother as she talks calmly and pleasantly to some man, and it is so good to sit beside her and just enjoy it.

But I am woken up that night by Mother's screaming and by Daddy's shouting about 'not performing your wifely duties', and I lie in bed cowering and ashamed that I don't get up to help her. Next morning Mother has a black eye, and later that year my little sister Georgia is born. She is beautiful. I have a birthday while Mother is in hospital with the new baby. I am seven years old and we listen to the broadcast of the Melbourne Cup on the wireless in the hospital. My horse, Windbag, wins the cup and Jennie's horse, Manfred, comes second. With our winnings Mother buys us new shoes, which I love, but Jennie is old enough to be furious that she couldn't spend her winnings in her own way (and also furious at my horse winning?).

Later still I will remember yet another birthday party. It is one that I resist remembering for a very long time, because I cannot bear it.

I am very small, and there are kids there, a cake with candles, lollies on a plate on the table. I take one and am smacked.

'Don't touch!' says Mother. 'They're not for you, they're for the family!'

And long before that, when Daddy has gone, or not yet come, Uncle George is the one who comes home every afternoon. He brings us ginger beer in a stone bottle, and chocolates, and a big sleeping-doll for me. He calls me his baby and brings me a gold chain bracelet with a heart with my name on it dangling from it, so I know who I am. And every day is a party. But Jennie says: 'It should have been mine! I'm the eldest!'

'Uncle gave it to me because I am his baby!' I say. 'He loves me!'

After that when Uncle comes, Mother says: 'Go out in the yard and play! He doesn't come to see you! He comes to see *me*!' And then Daddy comes, and Mother tells Uncle that I am Daddy's baby, and Uncle George goes away muttering: 'She should never have been allowed to see the light of day!'

And after that, for me the parties are over.

When Jock came home from the war, for a while all he wanted to do was party. He soon went through his deferred pay, drinking and partying with his similarly restless mates and the girls they picked up. When his leave was up, he was put in camp at Ballarat where, thin and grey-faced, he could never get warm.

'Colder than bloody Switzerland!' he growled. 'At least in Switzerland they knew it was cold and sealed their houses against it and provided heating. Here you could bloody die of it!'

Soon he was in and out of hospital with sinus trouble, for which they performed some hideously painful operation on his inflamed nasal membranes.

'Lot of bloody butchers!' he called the doctors, and a long and angry war between them and him ensued. Not long after he came home, he was taken off to hospital in the middle of one night screaming with pain from stones in the kidney.

'Worse than childbirth!' Daddy told me seriously when he was old and suffering from the same thing. I laughed heartlessly. 'How could you know?' I asked.

Jock was convinced that the doctors thought he was malingering to avoid being sent up to New Guinea, but eventually he passed several stones, one as big as Ayers Rock, which he produced in triumph and flourished at his next medical.

One of the doctors baited him.

'You can only use that stone once!' he said.

Jock himself was not troubled again by either the kidney stones or the doctors for a long time, but his confidences activated in me a long-dormant fear and distrust of doctors that I had till then been unaware of.

And if I was uneasy at home, Jock was not very easy to live with either. He confided to me that nobody was going to boss him round the way they did before he went to the war. I felt the same way as he did, but I included him among those who weren't going to boss me, and it didn't occur to me that he included me in his list of bosses. I was so preoccupied with my own troubles that I was astonished that he felt he had been bossed around — it had always seemed to me that he was Daddy's pet.

*   *   *

He is the one Daddy picks up at the gate of the primary school to take to town to keep him company at the movies for the afternoon.

'Don't mention this to your mother,' Daddy warns Jennie and me, as we stand big-eyed and envious at the gate, watching them go. And we never do.

Jock is the talkative one who is taken on trips to the country to keep Daddy company on his cake or lolly rounds. I go once, but I am poor company as we drive along roads too narrow for two cars to pass, with high dark mountains above and dark deep valleys below. I sit beside him in rigid silence and am never taken again.

Even more importantly, Jock is the one who is allowed out to play every day after school, while the girls have to stay home and help.

I have not yet heard Jennie's stories about them being belted with the buckle end of the razor strop when they were small. I have forgotten that Jock is the one who is bullied at home over his sums and called stupid, and that he is the one who gets the strap at school and at home, whereas at school I only got the strap once, when I got all my spelling wrong after I had been away sick, and I roared so loudly at the injustice of it that the teacher bought my silence with a boiled lolly from a big tin she kept for such contingencies. And secretly I thought she was stupid, because she gave Tommy Watts the strap every day for months for not getting his spelling right, and he didn't spell any better after all those strappings than he did before.

At home Daddy has never laid a hand on me *that I can remember*. I even feel this in some way as a deprivation. Jock, whom Daddy loves, gets hidings. I don't, therefore . . . ?

If the flat at Bairnsdale had seemed like bliss for me, life in Switzerland must have been even better for Jock. There, he was far from the war zone, he had no responsibilities but was decently housed, he ate better than he had for years, and his days were full of contract bridge, skiing and tobogganing at the best ski resort in the Alps, and Manette.

When the war in Europe ended, the internees were rushed back to Australia to defend us against the Japanese. Jock, who was skilled from long practice at rebellion against rules that did not suit him, jumped ship at Marseilles and somehow got through chaotic Europe to Switzerland in an attempt to persuade Manette to follow him back to Australia. But she was daunted by the prospect of life in that vast, alien, barbaric land where nobody spoke any of her languages, and she and Jock still conversed only in halting Italian. I wondered if she were mirroring his fears, as well as expressing her own. She refused to come.

Jock brought his rage home to a house shimmering with rages.

Even before he left for overseas there had always been bared-teeth hostility between Jock and Gladys, and it was no better now.

There was Gladys's rage at having three extra adults landed on her, none of whom wanted to be there, and none of whom she wanted there.

There was my rage just at being home, with no immediate prospect of getting out.

There was Jennie's rage when she came to visit — her long-standing rage against Gladys, and against me for not taking her part properly against Gladys and Mother.

Georgia, my little sister — but she was no longer my little sister but a beautiful young woman with huge eyes and a magnolia skin — had been in the A.W.A.S. for two years and was having an affair with a married man, a Catholic, who was wrestling with the problems of divorce. She was not pleased to be home either.

And what of Brian, the youngest? What were his rages? He never told me. The friction between him and Daddy never seemed to me to be as serious as it was with the older three. He was apprenticed as an electrician to a good man and, like me, his days were spent doing something he liked doing and did well. When he was ill one time, and suffering from the lung problems he had contracted as a result of working with asbestos as a young man (which eventually killed him), he told me: 'It was awful at home after you left, Emma,' and I was surprised and touched to hear that I had been missed.

But Jock had no prospects. After he was demobbed, the army had tested him and said he was very intelligent and could do a degree in engineering if he first reached a satisfactory standard in English. He enrolled at Taylor's Coaching College and enlisted my aid to teach him grammar which, he said, Taylor's couldn't teach for nuts.

I tried. I had taught boys in high schools before with some success, but with Jock I made no progress at all. It was fourteen years since his last formal education, and his schooldays had not been happy. And he didn't think much of my methods.

'What the fuck is the point of all this stuff anyway!' he roared.

I didn't have the sense — or was it the guts? — to say then what I would be able to say now: 'For you, the only point is that it will get you into the course you want to do!' Instead I floundered, and he exploded: 'You can't teach! You're a bloody stuck-up schoolmarm bitch! Just because you've got a degree you bloody think you know everything! You know nothing! You've got rocks in your head!'

And, up to a point, he was right. There was at least one rock in my head that I had not then succeeded in dislodging, a rock put there by Mother when she said: 'Education is for boys not for girls, and you can't both have it!' I knew I had it and I knew I had no right to it, but some part of me was determined to keep it for myself. So we both gave up. And his chance was lost.

Within two years Jock was married to a big blonde girl, whom I liked very much. He became an accountant and was extremely efficient, though because he was unqualified, he was not well paid.

My little sister left home and married her hero. I left home and married the brother of a university friend, who seemed everything I had wanted in a husband. He was conscientious and reliable and came from a family which seemed totally respectable. Jock's marriage lasted for five years, mine for twenty-eight.

But I am digressing. This is a chapter about Jock and me, and there are two stories I have to tell before it is complete.

The first is about the day I turned twenty-one, a very *non-party* day.

Mother and Daddy are both in bed with the flu, and they give me five shillings to put a birthday present on the lay-by. I suppose they wish me a happy birthday, but it doesn't feel much like one.

'When you're twenty-one you're on your own,' Daddy is fond of saying to his children, and I feel very much on my own.

At the railway station I hand over my student concession form for my monthly ticket to the porter at the window. As he starts to process it, he notices the date of birth. 'Why!' he says, with a big friendly grin, 'It's your birthday! Your twenty-first! Happy birthday!'

I grab my ticket, burst into tears, and flee.

At university that morning, a friend of mine is showing off her twenty-first-birthday present, a beautiful leather handbag stuffed with bank-notes. Melbourne University at that time is populated by the rich or the well-to-do, and the air has been thick with talk of parties and presents, necklaces and imported overcoats and trips overseas. One lucky boy gets a car. Even the hard-up seem to have gold watches. I get through the day somehow, without telling anyone it is my birthday. It is too shaming.

I'm getting the tea that night when Jock arrives home, thrusts a rather sweaty piece of tissue paper into my hand and says, watching me intently: 'Happy Birthday!'

Inside the tissue paper is a gold watch.

Later I will learn that he has sold his stamp collection at the Victoria market to get the money to pay for it, but at the time I do again what I seem to do best at the time: I burst into tears.

'If you're going to cry,' says Jock gruffly, 'you'd better give it back!' And we laugh and hug each other.

There are some stories that perhaps don't really belong in this book because they are about Jock when he was old, and his second wife had died, so he lived alone and had been in and out of hospital a lot.

After he had a colostomy, I used to drive over every second day for a while, taking him what we called meals on wheels. He suggested I come and live with him, but I valued my independence too much and I refused. As part of his rehabilitation he had to go for a walk every day, and as he was at first too shaky to go alone, I accompanied him. We always took the same route, where there were no roads to cross, walking a house or two further each day.

One day he said to me, with a hint of his old bossiness: 'I want to walk three more houses today.'

I knew he had a purpose, which he didn't explain, and next day it became apparent. He had been estimating in his head how far it was to his nearest watering hole, the pub on the corner.

When I called next day, Jock was going out. Two old mates had come to take him to the pub.

I stayed there, a little concerned, till I saw him staggering home — from weakness, I think, more than alcohol — with a look of fixed concentration on his face, a friend on each arm and a look of diabolical triumph on his face.

I shouted at his friends in pretended fury: 'How dare you bring my husband home drunk!' and we all laughed, and I went home confident he had a few more years in him yet.

The other story is one I had to learn from his son, who had heard the story from his father when he was old and close to death.

'He told it to me three times. He kept telling it to me,' said his son, 'and impressing on me that if anything happened to him, there was one story that was to be told at his funeral.'

The story is this one.

When Jock is in grade six, we dawdle home from school one day and Jock gets into a fight with another boy in a vacant allotment. After a while it seems obvious to me that Jock is getting the worst of it, and I take my cardboard case full of books and bop his opponent over the head with it. And we bolt.

What I remember Jock saying at the time is: 'Why didn't you stay out of it? I'd have beaten him easy!'

What he tells his son to say is: 'The other kids said: "Don't take Wiltshire on, or you'll have to take his sister on too!"'

And I was glad that that was the only story he wanted told. He could have chosen lots of worse ones!

PART TWO

ISADORA'S SCARF

As a university student I read somewhere the story of Isadora Duncan: a shadowy figure, very beautiful, a dancer, a woman of the world, *that sort,* as my father would say with a subtle mixture of admiration and contempt. I kept telling people this story, for some reason, till a friend said: 'You've told us that story twice before, and I don't believe it anyway. Nobody wears a scarf so long that it could catch in the wheels of a car and strangle her.'

I was silenced. I was easily silenced.

But somehow I was sure the story was true.

Now I am married, happily married, with a husband and three children and a cat and a dog and a garden, and quite sure the rest will be plain sailing. Jennie comes to stay. She is sick and confused and I think — God help me! — a change of air, as Mother would have said, might help her. And from then on her life becomes divided into two parts: *before I had my nervous breakdown* and *after I had my nervous breakdown.*

She tells me about the scarf.

When all the others are in bed asleep, my husband and the cat and the dog and the children are all asleep, she starts talking.

At first she talks about her husband, who understands nothing, who is more interested in collecting old Morris cars than he is in looking after the farm or her, who sometimes gets drunk, who is the cause of it all, who she says she hates. She talks till 4 a.m. She does not seem to need any comments from me, she just needs to talk. It is a need I understand only too well, so I just listen. It is a role in the family I have played before often enough — too often?

Then she begins to talk about her — about *our* — childhood, and I begin to be afraid.

'When you were two,' she says to me, 'you had a lovely nature and everybody loved you.' (It is not how I remember it!) 'I thought,' she says, 'that you were getting all the love that belonged to me. I was the eldest!' she says fiercely. 'It was mine by right!'

So one night, she tells me, while the grown-ups and their visitors were sitting at the table talking, she played doctors with me. She was the doctor, and I was the patient, lying on the floor behind the couch while she bandaged my neck with a scarf. She tied the scarf tighter and tighter round my neck till my gaspings and gurglings could no longer be ignored by the grown-ups, and Daddy came and released me.

Do I gasp at this? Recoil?

'You were all right!' she says impatiently. 'You weren't hurt!'

It is her story she is trying to tell, and she is coming to the important part, which is that no-one said anything to her, nobody blamed her or was angry or even seemed to mind. Daddy just laughed (*Not in front of the others, stupid*) and went back to the table and went on talking.

And Jennie was left dangling, somehow. She had not got what she wanted or needed.

One more night she talks, and that is the last.

She tells me the part she has needed, but not wanted, to tell.

She tells me how after the factory closed down, when she was sixteen and I was eleven, and she and Daddy were both out of work for a while, he would have intercourse with her on the bathroom floor while Mother was out shopping.

She blamed herself, of course. 'I was asking for it!' she says.

Mother came home and found them together.

'The bathroom floor!' I say to myself stupidly. *'Why the bathroom? That awful icy cold bathroom!'*

To her I say, and it is the only thing I say through all this: 'How horrible!'

All this, to me, till five o'clock in the morning, while my husband sleeps.

I will not believe it. She wouldn't do that. Daddy wouldn't do that. She's only saying that because she's off her head. And even if it were true, it's so long ago that it doesn't matter. And I push it away.

And now at last I enlist my husband — my husband, who early in my marriage, when I said simply: 'My father gave me a bad time when I was a kid,' had replied, equally simply: 'Don't give me that! I know Rex! Rex is a good bloke!'

Daddy is everybody's good bloke.

And I had been both relieved that I didn't have to explain — if I could! — what I meant by a bad time, and yet I felt somehow betrayed too. I had listened to *his* family stories and taken his part.

So now I don't tell my husband what Jennie has been saying, I just say: 'I can't handle this alone. She needs a doctor, a psychiatrist, I think.'

At this time in my life, psychiatrists are as remote from my experience as men from Mars. My husband, who can hardly have been sleeping very soundly through all this, agrees.

We send for the doctor, and it is not the man from the local clinic who usually attends my children who comes, but a stranger. I tell him something of what has been happening.

'I think she needs a psychiatrist,' I say.

But the G.P. reassures us.

'No! No!' he says. 'She doesn't need a psychiatrist. I have a brother who's a psychiatrist. I can handle it. Just get this prescription made up. I'll be back in the morning.'

So we give her the pills and she sleeps all day, and next night we go to bed early, exhausted, but she is refreshed and ready for more. She keeps coming into my room, and when I resist waking she tries to force my eyelids open.

'Emma! Emma! Wake up! Wake up!'

I am firm. I take her back to bed, like one of the children. I give her another pill.

But she comes back, and back, and finally she comes shrieking: 'Emma! Emma! Wake up! There are men in cars, out the front, and they're coming to take me away!'

I stay calm. I make soothing noises. I take her to the front door, switch on the outside light, show her our empty, moonlit, dead-end street. 'Look, Jennie. No men. No cars.'

I take her back to bed.

But her 'Wake up, Emma, wake up!' has chipped my shell. I have heard it before from her, those identical words, and the past which I have smothered so successfully for so long begins to break its cover and will not be denied.

I sit up at night now, till I am sure she's asleep, and — feeling like a mad-woman — I pile up at the door of my sleeping children's bedroom a collection of saucepans and lids, so poised that they can't be touched without falling, without making a terrible clatter. I know that if a sound comes from their room, I will wake, as I have always woken at the slightest cry from one of them, and I will be in there before the cry is even finished. Then I go to bed myself.

*　　*　　*

And now I am myself at risk. I am Humpty Dumpty (*Dumb Humpty*, as my youngest calls him) sitting on my wall. I will not fall down. I have three children, and there is no-one I trust to look after them as I trust myself. *I will not fall down.* I am perched on my wall, my shell cracked in so many places that if I make any move, if I breathe, if I speak and start saying — — — all my juices will start flowing out, and all the king's horses and all the king's men will never be able to put me together again. (*As soon as she warms up, she'll bleed to death.*)

Stay cool, Emma, stay cool!

And I begin to long for her to be gone, feeling like (Daddy's phrase) a two-faced bitch, so that I can go back to that ordinary everyday existence, where the most important things are getting the tea, weeding the garden, comforting the children, and they are all within my power. Now, when I eventually get to sleep, I don't want to wake up. It is too hard. I don't think I can do it any more. I can't say what I long to say to Jennie: 'Go back to your house. Go back to your husband. Go anywhere. I can't listen any more.' I can't send her home till she is ready to go. There are too many Jennies jostling round in my head for that.

There is the Jennie who fed me a bottle a long time ago when Mother could not or would not get up to me, after a neighbour's husband, who'd come at her request to unblock the kitchen sink for her, had raped her and left her pregnant with Ronald George.

There is the Jennie who punched a girl called Bessie

in the belly for telling on me in grade one, after I had taken an arum lily out of a lady's garden to give to my then idol, the teacher Miss Lord. Could she really have been called Lord? Yes, she was, but lord or no lord she put a label on me saying THIEF, and I had to stand in the corner till playtime, when I'd gone out bawling to Jennie, who'd exacted her revenge. Bessie's mother, Mrs Blessington, had come up after tea and complained to Mother about Jennie hitting her.

'I don't mind you hitting her, and I admit she deserved it, but next time, *Don't hit her in the belly!*'

There is the Jennie — with much more gumption than me — who made toffee and chocolate fudge when Mother was out and, when we heard the car, organised Jock and me into lightning clean-ups before they could park the car and get inside.

There is the Jennie who brilliantly outsmarted Jock and me when we were playing up on her once when Mother and Daddy had gone out leaving her in charge, as they too often did.

She has washed up and we are supposed to dry, but we jack up on her. Somehow we manage to lock her in the dining room. Soon there are strange noises, clankings and rattlings, strange moaning, sobbing noises. It is Jennie.

'There are men in here,' she quavers. 'They're going to take me away! Go out the back and let the dog off the chain!'

Out we rush. While we stand fumbling with the catch on Nick's chain, we are frozen into immobility as a ghostly figure comes round the side, clothed in white from head to toe (the honey-comb quilt off my bed) and making moaning and clanking noises.

It is not my finest hour.

I am inside the back door in a flash, abandoning Jock to his fate. Soon there is banging on the back door and Jock calling: 'Unlock the door, you dope! It was only Jennie! Let us in!' They are killing themselves laughing, but it will take me quite a while to be convinced enough to open the door!

I have had experiences before with someone who was supposed to have returned from the dead!

There is another Jennie who explained to me what the red-black mess in my navy blue school pants was when I was twelve, and assured me I wouldn't bleed to death. I don't remember the details of her sex education, but afterwards it seemed safe to bleed freely. I was delighted to learn that I was now a woman and could have babies, though before then I had for some reason been convinced that that would not be possible. But I left a smear of blood (accidentally? on purpose?) on the lavatory seat, and Mother, who made no other reference to my menstruation, warned me to be more careful. 'We wouldn't want the men to know,' she said. The men in the house at that time were Harry and Daddy and, no, I didn't want Daddy to know. So menstruation became another thing to be secretive about.

There is the Jennie who held my hand as in mutual terror we raced to turn off the light after reading the books about ghosts. And there is the Jennie who had all the boyfriends and could look like a film star, and who cried in the night, and hated God.

This Jennie — the Jennie with the scarf, the Jennie on the bathroom floor — I can't yet get my head around.

Too many Jennies, too many Emmas.

My father turns up, unexpected, uninvited, to stay the night. Coincidence? I don't think I believe in coincidence.

It is not his usual fortnightly visit with Gladys, when we eat a good meal and sit around having relations-type conversations in which nothing much of any importance is said, or even watching T.V. This time he comes alone, without Gladys, and he stays the night. And what he says is not just surface talk.

'Get rid of her. Send her away!' he says, with some energy. 'You've got your own nice home and family; she'll only make trouble!'

How could he? His eldest daughter!

I don't say anything. I don't tell him anything. I don't ask him anything. I don't want to know anything. I long to be alone.

Next morning I get up, and Jennie is off to talk to the doctor, not to me any more, and my father is still there.

My smallest daughter, aged two, she of the loving heart and the bright eyes and the ready chuckle, is sitting on his knee in the kitchen, chattering and stroking his dimple, the 'hole in his face', as that other little girl, long ago, had done. I snatch her off his knee, send her sharply out to play.

It is what I thought then, and quickly suppressed, that will send me off later in search of a psychiatrist myself.

My father goes home.

After several weeks Jennie too goes home, sort-of reconciled to her husband.

I still visit my father every month, always *en famille*, never again alone. He will come back once a fortnight too, but never without Gladys.

And I will never leave any of my children alone with him again.

I am now Persephone, part of me alive and joyous in the world, among the flowers, among my family; the other half, as soon as they go to school or to work, dead and imprisoned. There is no Orpheus to rescue me with his music. But like Orpheus, I dare not look back.

BAMBOO

For years I had some bamboo in a tub. It softened an ugly brick corner of the house quite charmingly until it began suddenly — no, it had been happening for years — I suddenly *noticed* that it was bursting out of the sides of its container. Eventually the confining steel bands round the sides burst through their studs and the whole thing disintegrated. I did not consciously remember the warnings that had made me confine it in a tub in the first place, but when I broke it up I threw most of it out and replanted some healthy shoots in a little rectangle of garden with a brick wall behind it and cement paths all round it, so it could not run rampant. Almost before I had put the tools away, it was on the move. It crept beyond the garden, broke up bits of the path in front, and crept under the thicker wider path into the front garden where it began to sprout vigorously.

Memory is like that.

After Jennie's breakdown, the me that had for so long been satisfied, even eager, not to be noticed, that had refused to remember, began to shake my tub and force her way out. I got a grip on myself, as I had done all my life, did what needed doing, cooking, washing, cleaning, gardening, and hoped no-one noticed the inner turmoil, but while my husband was at work and the children at school, I sometimes took to my bed for the afternoon and gave in to anxiety and black depression and felt I was going mad. And because of what had flooded into my mind when I saw my daughter on Daddy's knee, I knew I had to do something.

A recollection from my university days suggested a way out.

In my Diploma of Education year, I had attended a series of free lectures given by an American woman, a Dr Anita Muhl, who was, I think, a criminologist and a psychiatrist. Her lectures were so fascinating that students, both graduate and undergraduate, of both sexes and all disciplines, flocked to hear her, filling the seats, packing the aisles, standing along the steps of the passageways to the top of the large public lecture theatre, cramming into the spaces around the doors and craning their necks from outside in those pre-speaker-system days, trying to catch her every word.

Two things she said stayed with me. One was that she was amazed, when she came to Australia, to find that the favourite indoor sport was hitting the kids. And I had made another of my resolutions: that I would never hit my children, if ever I were lucky enough to have any.

The other thing was a story she told as one of her failures, of a black girl (like me, the wrong colour!)

who had come to her for help. The girl kept talking about blood, and after one session she went away and murdered her whole family.

'I was working too hard and was stressed,' said Dr Muhl, 'and I know that if I'd listened more carefully, I could have prevented it.'

Am I in danger of murdering someone? Have I already murdered someone? I know that sometime, way back, I have done something dreadful, and so far I have resisted knowing what it was. After Jennie's breakdown I decide, no matter what dreadful thing it is I have done, I can go no longer without finding out. I need someone who will *listen* to me.

And the child in me that I had kept still and invisible for years was beginning to move, to shift, to kick, to push and to thrust, to demand a way out, more space, more freedom. This child was demanding to know the truth.

Without discussing it with my husband, I rang my gynaecologist, who had seen me through three difficult births and who I felt was too competent, too responsible, too reliable, to send me to some crackpot, some *Svengali*, some *Rasputin* (some Mesmer?) and asked him to refer me to a psychiatrist. I am amazed still at my good sense in taking such a step, and in asking for a name from the only man I knew who might have the sophistication to know who to recommend.

My husband, when I told him what I had done, hit the roof.

'You're my wife!' he said, in grief and anger, as though like Caesar's wife I must be beyond reproach.

'People in our position don't do such things!' he said. 'You've got a new house and a new car, and you're just looking for another way of spending money! It's just a question of pulling yourself together!'

Except for the bit about spending money, which I knew wasn't true, I'd been saying such things to myself for years. Now I knew I must have help. I rang to make an appointment.

A rather querulous receptionist said the doctor was very busy. He was not taking any new patients and not making any more appointments. Reluctantly she made one for me in three weeks. (*Nothing like pulling out the welcome mat! Stupid bitch! I could be dead in three weeks!* this new melodramatic me raged inwardly.)

The day of my appointment I dithered around and missed the last train that would get me there on time. (*I don't want to go!*)

I took a taxi — an unheard-of extravagance. (*I'm going! No matter what John says, I'm going!*)

In a waiting-room furnished with beautiful period furniture, I was kept waiting for almost an hour. (*After I've paid for a taxi so I wouldn't keep him waiting! My time is just as valuable to me as his time is to him!*) And as I waited, I became at first enraged, then terrified, and then preternaturally aware.

The doctor came and ushered me into his study — a couple of chairs, a desk (*desks mean lawyers,*

policemen, headmasters, headmistresses) on which sat
a pipe (*he's a doctor and yet he smokes — a pipe like
those pipes Daddy used to smoke, long ago, but
stopped because he kept biting the stems off*), a big
leather-bound blotting-paper pad (*he's rich*), and a pair
of horn-rimmed spectacles like my mother wore in her
later years.

But he asked, quite gently: 'How can I help you?'

And as though he had touched a spring, I began
to talk.

I talked, not saying any of the neat things I had
planned to say — that I was depressed, though I had a
good husband and lovely children so I had no reason
to be depressed — but about Jennie's breakdown, and
about feeling like a two-faced bitch, and about Daddy
and Jennie in the bathroom, and the pots and pans I'd
put at the bedroom door, and I began to cry. Oh
shame! I began to cry, after I had resolved? promised?
sworn? never to cry again. And as soon as I cried, like
a tap being turned off, I stopped talking.

He sent me off to a psychologist for some tests. (At
school and university I did tests all the time, did well
at them, excelled at them — so why should the mere
mention of tests throw me into a spin?) I babbled to
the psychologist about what I saw in a series of ink-
blots, and they sent me what seemed an astronomical
bill which made my husband roar again and say he
wouldn't pay it, and though he later relented, I felt
again that he was right, that people in our position
couldn't do such things. Yet I knew I had to have help.

So without discussing with him any further, I went and got myself a relieving job for three weeks, teaching Leaving Certificate English at Mount Scopus College, working all day and half the night because I hadn't even read some of the texts I had to revise for the approaching term exams.

I paid the first bill.

When I went back to the analyst, he laid it on the line for me. I was suffering, he said, from an anxiety neurosis.

'It is an illness,' he said, 'and like most illnesses, it can be cured.' I would need to go to him regularly for two years; I would feel better for a time, but it would be a mistake to leave as soon as I felt better; I would need to stay until the treatment was completed.

I was appalled. I could never afford to go for two years!

'My husband's a teacher,' I said, 'we don't have that kind of money!'

I had hoped, I suppose, for some swift confession, like going to a priest, with immediate absolution. But full of rage and pain and distrust as I was, when he said it could be cured he had given me hope, and I would not let go.

So I answered an advertisement in *The Age*, and like a gift from heaven I got a job at a prestigious girls' school, teaching Latin through the school on two-thirds time.

I had good references and my qualifications were just right. I didn't just get the job, I was snapped up by the headmistress, who said she must interview the other applicants for whom she'd made appointments but assured me that the job was mine. She was a woman after my own heart, who told me that the philosophy of the school was to cater not only for the academically gifted, but for all girls, whatever their capabilities.

'And we're not just the snob-shop of Toorak, as some of our detractors say,' she said, 'but our academic results are excellent too.'

I couldn't believe my luck.

I could afford the treatment.

There were rumblings in the family, not only at me getting such a good job (*She'll never get a job at her age after so long away from it!*), but about the psychiatrist, who turned out to be not a psychiatrist but an analyst. I didn't know the difference — perhaps psychiatrists gave pills, analysts didn't?

I begin to panic. I'm very afraid.

I go away and buy myself some Relaxatabs and take a few. I come out in a rash all over my body. The skin specialist I am sent to tells me the rash is caused by a drug. I am outraged. I have taken no drugs! But he ignores my protests — throws long lists of drugs at me — hammers away at me till I'm really angry — No! No! NO! until he comes to Relaxatab. And I stop him, say weakly, 'Yes. A few Relaxatabs.'

He smiles. 'Don't take any more,' he says. 'You're allergic to them.'

I will take no more pills! I have always hated them!

I went back to the analyst (who doesn't prescribe pills) and for a while I was talking again, and just to be able to open my mouth and speak freely and be listened to for the first time in my life was for a time an enormous relief. I told him two things that I later realised were contradictory. First I said: 'I was the baby, for seven years, until my little sister was born.' Later I told him about being very small, just big enough to look over the side of his bassinet at my baby brother. 'His name,' I said, 'was Ronald George, but I called him Onda Dord.'

But I was not listening to myself at the time and I didn't notice the discrepancy.

I told him too about being taken by ambulance to either the Children's Hospital or the Alfred when I was very small.

'What happened to you?' he asked.

'Nothing,' I said, in sudden alarm. 'Nothing happened. I don't remember.'

'I'd better be careful,' he said to himself. 'There are some contradictions here. This may not be true!' (*Another one who thinks it's all lies?*) But he asked me what my name had been before I was married, went off and checked the hospital records, and when he read the extent and the horrific nature of my injuries he was appalled, and amazed that I had lived.

'This kid should be dead!' he said to himself, and with my newly re-awakened awareness I heard him. And at some deep level I filed away the recognition that he had checked it out, and that it was true, and that he knew that it was true. And like Jennie's 'Wake up! Emma, wake up!', his words are words I have heard before in another life.

And though this gives me hope, as his claim that my illness could be cured gave me hope, I am caught in a dangerous undertow. An undertow, I understand, is a current moving below the surface in a contrary direction to the surface current. By going against John's wishes, I seem to be putting at risk that life I have built up, that now-me, who is John's wife, the mother of his children, the woman of the brick house, the car, the good job.

The surface current supports me in wanting to preserve my marriage at all costs, and in my realisation that I must have help — I can't do this on my own. This man, I believe, is a good man, a specialist in his field, recommended by my gynaecologist, another top man in his field. The analyst has done the work of checking the records, he has seen the evidence, he knows it is true. This knowledge was a load off my mind, but it also brought me undone; a process which Jennie's recollections about the bathroom floor had started. By looking at the evidence in the hospital records, he has lifted the lid on the Pandora's box that I have been sitting on for almost forty years, and what flies out is too monstrous, too obscene, for me to deal with.

Who was she, this kid in the hospital bed, so badly damaged that the doctor — everybody — thought she should be dead? She is not me!

How did she get there?

What happened to her?

'What happened to her?' my husband asked Jock.

And Jock answered with the family myth: 'Nothing happened! She made it all up. She'd be dead if all that had happened to her! She's just bunging on an act as a way of getting a bit of attention. This bloke's just after her money.'

Jennie said, angrier than I ever remember her: 'You're not to talk about me!'

And Daddy said with one of his slow, sly smiles: 'You've got children now, Em. You'd better be very careful. And the leopard does not change his spots.'

Is it a threat, almost? ('Don't be silly, Em!' I tell myself. 'You're getting paranoid!')

I am not going to put my children at risk! The undertow takes over and I clam up.

I say to the doctor: 'I can't talk any more.'

The doctor doesn't talk the family lingo to me; he doesn't say: 'There's no such word as can't! Of course you can bloody talk! Just do it, and be quick about it!'

He says, as though he believes me when I say I can't talk: 'If you can't talk, perhaps you can write it down?'

And though I have not yet remembered the first time when Jennie said, with her terrible urgency: 'Emma! Emma! Wake up!', I know I cannot write it down or everything will be spoiled. If I write it, as I wrote something then, nothing will ever be the same again. Everything will be spoiled. So I tell him I can't write it either.

Describing this time to one of my daughters when at last I could bear to talk about it, I said I must have seemed to him a patient sent from hell; I wouldn't talk, and I wouldn't go away, and yet I shrieked at him: 'If you can't help me, find me someone who can! I have three children and they may be at risk.'

Of what, I did not know.

And he is stymied. He sees my need, and he is too decent, too professional, to kick me out, but until I can talk, or write, he can do little to help me.

He puts me in a group, and at his suggestion I pay at a greatly reduced rate, but I see it as charity again and I cannot bear it. I get the job and insist on paying at the full rate.

The doctor is alarmed on many counts. He realises Jung says that analysis is not successful for women over forty. (*So who's Jung? And is this another way of saying that once a woman hits forty she's over the hill?*) He knows I am reading his mind, as I think he is reading mine, and is reluctant to put a psychic in a group. Finally he is worried that it may all be too much for me.

But I have set something in motion which I cannot recall, and I have to see it through.

Eventually I am saved, because at last I will begin to take the analyst's advice and listen to that inner voice, that small voice, my own voice, which I have smothered for so long, and to finish those sentences that I was never allowed to finish. Without him as some sort of lighthouse beacon in the distance, I would have given in

— often did give in — to black depression and despair. So though I am not yet ready to trust anyone with my story, and though I resist as though my life depends on it his every attempt to break up my turf, to free and prune my pot-bound roots, the process has begun and eventually cannot be halted. At some level, I know that this man, this analyst, is someone who can help, and that he cares what happens to me, and in spite of myself he may be able to see me through.

And the bamboo begins to shoot.

SO WHAT HAPPENED TO
SATURDAY AND SUNDAY?

IT'S NO use.

I can't remember. It was all so long ago!

Nobody should have to remember things like that!

But at last I do.

I remember what happened when I was too young to remember.

I remember what I can't possibly remember, because I was only a baby.

I remember.

I am in a different place. With one eye — the other eye is covered up — I start to see the room I am in. The walls are made of curtains. The ceiling is a long, long way up.

I float away.

*   *   *

When I float back, there are people in white dresses, like a picture of heaven. Is this heaven? Heaven's where you go when you're dead.

I float away.

Mother is in a chair beside my bed, in the room with the curtain walls. She is crying and crying. Mothers are allowed to cry.

'Now I'll never get rid of them!' she sobs.

I float away.

When I come back, two of the ladies — angels? — are talking.

'You'd better get a wriggle on,' says one. 'Matron comes early on Mondays!'

Monday? It is not Monday. After Friday come Saturday and Sunday. Where have Saturday and Sunday gone? Jock goes to school, and he says it's very important to get the days right.

I hear voices. From a long way off. From another time.

Someone at the back door, knocking and banging and calling out: 'Is everything all right? I heard the dog barking and then I thought I heard screaming.'

(*One sound out of you and I'll kill the pair of you!*)

Daddy's smiling voice: 'No! No! Had the gramophone playing too loud! Those screeching sopranos, you know what they're like! I've just turned it off. Sorry about that!'

Daddy is looking for my heart. He can't find my heart.

'Dead as a doornail!' he says.

'Light the copper! Have to soak them in cold water first! Get the blood out! Lug her downstairs! Get rid of the pocket-knife! Quick! Into the dunny-can! Night-cart comes in the morning!'

'How am I to get rid of her? If I had a car . . . I could take her to Edwards Lake and tie a rock around her and pitch her in. I could put her in one of those wardrobe drawers. Have to cut her legs off. I can't do anything tonight — I'm too tired. I'll think about that in the morning.'

Mother's voice. 'My God! My God! What have you done?'

'Touch that phone and you're dead!' says Daddy.

* * *

More voices.

'God, what a stink!' says the doctor. 'Clean her up. I can't touch her till she's cleaned up.'

'She's better off dead,' says Mother, as she pushes my head under the water in the bath.

'What's going on here?' says the doctor, from the bathroom door.

'She slipped,' says Mother.

'She'll be dead before she gets to the hospital!' says the doctor.

I am in a sort of truck. I am on a kind of bed. My face is right up near the roof. There is a bell ringing and ringing as we go along.

'God!' says another doctor. 'She's dead! And thank God for that! I don't want to have to deal with that! Put her in a bag and take her away!'

Why does he say I'm dead? I'm not dead. I know I'm not dead. When you're dead, you can't feel anything. Daddy said so. When they put me in the bag and hung me upside down, I began to hurt. I hurt in my chest.

Daddy told me a story about when he dug up the baby. He said that when he dug him up, he dug up the beans first, in little blocks, then the baby. He said he put the baby on a towel, then put the blocks of beans back. You couldn't tell they'd been moved.

He said the baby was all rotten and bits of him were gone.

'Where was the rest of him?'

'Gone. Once you're dead, you just rot away.'

'Does it hurt?'

'Once you're dead, you don't feel a thing.'

'Did he know he was dead?'

'Once you're dead, you can't think. You don't know anything.' And Daddy laughs. 'When I put him in the ground, he wasn't even dead!'

I am not dead. I am hurting! My eyes are closed, but I can *think*.

I call out from my head: '*I am not dead! Get me down!*'

'She's dead! She couldn't call out. From what I heard, her mouth and jaw are too badly damaged ever to speak again.'

But from my head I call out again: '*Get me down! I'm not dead! Get me down!*'

'I s'pose I'd better get her down and examine her,' says the doctor.

* * *

'God! She's alive! I'll have to do something! But whatever I do, she'll die anyway.'

'Why don't you just let her die? She'll never be any good after this!'

'Hippocratic oath: *Do no harm.*'

'Let her die!' says the matron. 'I need the bed! I'm not going to waste a bed on that! I've already got more children than I can handle, but they have at least some hope of surviving. This one will die in a few days anyway!'

'She's alive! The hospital says she's alive!'

'I tell you she's dead! *I did all the tests!* No pulse! No heartbeat! I struck a match near her eyes and she didn't blink! I held a mirror to her mouth — no breath! She's dead, I tell you!'

'If she comes back, I'll do it again! And next time I'll make a job of it. Give me two minutes alone with her behind those screens! I can fix her with a pillow! No-one will be any the wiser!'

I float away from all the voices. I am never coming back.

Loud frightening voices in the corridor pull me back.

Daddy is shouting at a man. He starts to shout at the doctor: 'This bastard won't let me in to see my own daughter!'

'I'm in charge here!' says the doctor. 'Your daughter is too ill to have any visitors!'

It is nice Daddy now. 'Sorry to get upset! Thought he was just being officious! I just wanted to see my daughter. My little daughter!' His voice falters. 'She's the baby, you know! After all that's happened, you know!'

'No more visitors!' says the doctor.

Nobody comes.

They are cruel. I want a drink. They won't give me one. They put ice in my mouth instead. I don't want ice! I want a drink!

'She can't swallow,' says the doctor. 'A drink would drown her.'

They cut my throat and stick something in it and I am not thirsty any more.

I am very cold.

'As soon as she warms up, she'll bleed to death,' says the doctor, 'before we can even start to work on her.'

'They reckon Saturday night was the coldest November night since they started taking records,' says another doctor. 'That's what saved her.'

'We'll pack her in ice,' says the other doctor.

*   *   *

They put something over my nose and I am asleep. While I sleep, I hear them talking. They are cutting me open — making holes in me!

It is all happening again!

They take something out of me called a spleen, so I won't bleed to death.

They stick needles in me.

'Morphia,' they say, 'for the pain.'

It gives me a lovely feeling. No more pain.

When I wake up, the pain is back.

'More!' I say. 'More!'

'Not till four o'clock!' they say. 'Not till the doctor says. You'll be a drug addict if you have it whenever you want it.'

'Put the screens around her!' they say. 'Don't let the other children see her! It would frighten them!'

'Makes you sick to look at her!' they say.

'What an animal!' they say.

'They say it was her father,' says the little nurse who has to wash it all off. 'She must have done something really terrible for him to do that to her!'

'No feeling, no movement in that left leg,' they say. 'A clot. If it's not gone by morning, the leg will have to come off.'

Why does everyone want to cut my legs off?

* * *

'I never even touched her! She must have been lying there like that when I came home! Out with the boys, you know! Drunk as a skunk I was! Spewed all over the bed. Had to wash the sheets this morning. My wife would kill me if she came home and found a mess like that!

'My dog! Why would I kill my own dog? He was devoted to me!

'I never even touched her! I was so drunk I could hardly walk, let alone do that! I'm a respectable married man with a wife and three children! I wouldn't do something like that! Someone's come in the back door — it's never locked — followed her from the station and done that to her!

'It's my daughter who's put you up to that, I'll bet. She told people I killed the baby, and he died of natural causes, and I've got the paper to prove it!'

The woman won't testify! They're in it together. I'll get him for this, if it's the last thing I do!

But I know. The policeman's wrong. *Daddy didn't do it. He wouldn't say he didn't if he did, or God would strike him dead. Mother said so.*

* * *

'As long as I keep my head, and keep my mouth shut, they can't prove a thing. But I'm going to have to watch my step — give up the booze and the pills. One mistake and I'm done for! I'll never touch anyone in the house again! It's too dangerous.'

The voices drift in and they drift out.

It is a hospital I am in. Like the one Mother went to to have the baby. They look after you when you are sick. The curtain walls have gone. It is a long room I am in now, with two long rows of beds, one on each side, and a child in every bed. Some have bandages on their heads, like me. Some have their legs up in the air, tied to stick things. We all have to lie in bed all day and look at the ceiling. No-one comes except nurses and doctors. They always do things that hurt me terribly, but not on purpose. I think they're trying to make us all better. At visiting hour on Sundays, the other mothers come. My mother does not come. At night we get medicines to make us go to sleep. But there is a lady — the night nurse — who sits near the door at night with a light on her desk, so no-one can get in or out without her seeing. When all the other kids are asleep, I go to sleep too.

* * *

It is Christmas.

'She can't stay here!' says the matron. 'She'll have to go home!'

'I can't send her home to that!' says the doctor.

'Well, she can't stay here! I've got no staff over Christmas, and she's only a charity patient, after all!'

'I should have let her die!' says the doctor. 'She's never going to be any good after this!'

He comes home with me in the truck thing with the bed in it. It is called an ambulance. The bell doesn't ring.

'I'll hold you responsible for her,' he says. 'If anything happens to her, I'll hold you responsible. She won't be like other girls after this. She won't ever be able to do anything with those hands. She won't be able to read or write, or go to work, or marry and have children. She'll always need a lot of looking after. Don't let her look in the mirror. After Christmas we'll have her back in the hospital and fix those scars. Get rid of the stitches.'

The man says to me: 'Don't talk to that doctor any more. I'm the one who's in charge here!'

They have brought me to the wrong place. This is not my family. This is not our house. There are no stairs. They have sent me back to the wrong house. There is a man who looks like Daddy, but he has no moustache. There is a lady who looks like Mother, but her hair is cut short and she wears funny short dresses. There is a boy who looks like Jock, but Jock had a big gap where his front teeth had fallen out. This boy has two big teeth in the front. He can't be Jock.

'That's not our sister!' says the boy.

'That's not your daughter!' says the man. 'That's someone else's kid they've palmed off onto you!'

'Keep the blinds down! If anyone sees those stitches, they'll know that she didn't fall down the stairs!'

The boy comes in to look at me.

I stay asleep when anyone comes in.

At night I wake up screaming. There is no morphia. 'Nobody can put up with that!' says the man. 'If she goes on like that when she goes back to the hospital, those doctors will give her a pill that will shut her up for ever. I've seen it in the army.'

The girl comes in. She brings me a mirror.

'Have a look at yourself!' she says.

I look in the mirror. That is not me. The face has lines of red sores like railway lines, covered with brown stuff, the sting-y stuff, all over it. The head has no hair. I don't look that! I am *not* like that. It is ugly. It can't be me. *It is not me!*

I swim away again and close my eyes. I do not want to wake up.

THE FIRST WRITING
LESSON

I AM remembering.

I am remembering things before the hospital.

I am remembering the first time I wrote something.

I am remembering the first time Jennie said: 'Emma, wake up!'

It is the middle of the night. Jennie is shaking me.

'Emma! Emma! Wake up!' she is crying. 'They're killing the baby! You've got to go down and stop them! Emma! Wake up! Daddy wants you! Wake up!'

I wake up, and in my new birthday nightie with the pink ribbon bows I go in my bare feet along the polished boards, down the three steps towards the ribbon of light shining from Mother's bedroom. It is my birthday. I am three years old today.

My heart is singing. I have only heard three of

Jennie's words. *Daddy wants me!* Daddy never wanted me before!

Then I hear the screaming. Mother is screaming, the baby is screaming and Daddy is shouting: 'You're going to be in this too!' and as I get to the door I see he is holding Mother's arm so that when he sticks the scissors into the baby, she is doing it too.

And I — *yes, I* — say in a strange, loud, clear voice: 'Daddy! Stop it!'

He stops. He turns to me and stares.

'I'm not having a three-year-old kid telling me what to do!' he says, and he comes at me.

'What have you done?' says Daddy.

'Look at your hands!' says Daddy.

'Look at your nightgown!' says Daddy.

'What have you done?' says Daddy.

'Watch my watch!' says Daddy. He is laughing and talking to himself. 'Bloke called Mesmer invented it. It's called hypnotism. Saw it in the army. Shell-shock hospital. You can make them say anything you tell them to.'

He waves his watch on its long gold chain back and forward in front of me.

'Repeat after me!' he says and because of the cigarette, I do it. I say in a strange voice what he tells me to say: 'I stabbed the baby because I was jealous.'

The doctor comes and mends the baby.

Then Daddy says to me: 'Tell the doctor what you told me.'

And I say again in my different voice: 'I stabbed the baby because I was jealous.'

I keep saying it over and over again till Daddy says: 'That's enough.'

The doctor looks from me to Mother, to Daddy, and back to me in my bloodstained nightie, me with the blood on my hands (*Something funny going on here!*), and he says to Mother: 'Clean her up and change her nightie. I'll give her something to make her sleep, and in the morning with a bit of luck she won't remember a thing about it.' And he sticks a needle in me and I go to sleep.

But in the morning Daddy gets me up before Jennie and Jock go to school, and makes me stand up and say it all over again in front of them. And after the others have gone, he takes a pencil and says: 'Write what I say.'

I can't do real writing, not till next year when I'll be old enough to go to school, but he holds my hand with the pencil in it and it makes marks on the paper.

'I'll keep this,' he says, 'so everyone will know you stabbed the baby. Now you're an accessory after the fact. And if anyone finds out, they'll put you in gaol for the rest of your life. So if you know what's good for you, you'll keep your mouth shut.'

Now everybody thinks I stabbed the baby, and I no longer know for sure whether I did or not. He wouldn't make me say it if it wasn't true. He wouldn't burn me with the cigarette, he wouldn't do such things, he wouldn't he wouldn't he wouldn't — not my Daddy.

And when Daddy is gone, Mother says to me: 'It's best if you take the blame, or he'll kill the lot of us. Forget it. Pretend it never happened, or we can't go on.'

Afterwards when the baby dies, Jennie says: 'It's all your fault! You should have stopped them. You're the one nobody wants!'

I push it away. But now it is no good. I can't push it all away as I have always done. It is like when I began to cry when the baby died. Once I started crying, I couldn't stop. Now I have started remembering and I can't stop.

The next thing I remember is about Jock. My big brother. He's only a year older than me so he's not as big as Jennie who's five years older, and Mother always says to me and Jennie: 'Look after Jock.'

When he was little, he was always in trouble.

He can't resist the water. He climbs up and turns the tap on over the wash-troughs or the gully-trap, or turns on the hose and floods the back yard and wallows in the mud, and though Mother comes out and slaps him and shuts him out, he kicks at the back door and roars so loudly that Mother is afraid of what the neighbours will say and lets him in.

It is my fault.

'Everything was all right till you came,' he says to me.

'She's my mother, not yours!' he says.

'I thought she was everybody's mother.'
'Well, you're wrong!' he says.

I am lying on the ground in the backyard. Jock has pulled my dress halfway up and my bloomers halfway down. He spits on my stomach, rubs the spit round and round, and says: 'Now we're married and you have to do what I tell you for the rest of your life.' (So that's what being married means!)

He bangs me on the head with half a brick that is lying there; I begin to roar and Mother comes out. I have pulled my dress down and my pants up, but I tell on him about the brick.

'Never did!' says Jock angrily. 'She tripped and fell and hit her head on that brick! Never touched her! She's a little liar!'

Mother believes him. She never believes me. All she says is: 'Look at your dress! Look what you've done to your nice clean dress!'

Jock goes to school. He hates it.

Jennie says: 'No wonder! They gave him the strap on the first day and shut him in the ink cupboard!'

He goes off bawling every morning with his hands stuck in the top of his pants to keep them warm.

'My wegs are waching!' he cries.

'I've got a stomach-ache!' he cries.

I feel very sorry for him.

But Mother says he has to go.

'If you don't go to school, the truant officer will get you. And they'll put me in gaol for not making you go!' she says.

So Jennie drags him off, still crying. He has been going to school for a whole year and he still can't read or write or do his sums. Daddy tries to teach him, after tea.

'Repeat after me,' says Daddy. (*I don't think I will like school, either.*) 'Two and two are four, two and two are four,' and Jock repeats it over and over again.

'Now, how much are two and two?'

'Four.'

'Now! Three and two are five,' over and over.

'Now. How much are three and two?'

'Five.'

'Good. And how much are two and two?'

'Five.'

And Daddy goes mad.

Much later the analyst will explain to me why, for Jock, two and two always made five, and I was the fifth.

I don't go to school for a long time. Was it before or after — ? What?

I don't remember.

At first when I go to school, I am very scared because of the strap and the ink cupboard. But we have a kind lady called Miss Lord, who doesn't have a strap, and no-one gets sent to the ink cupboard. We don't use ink or pencils. Instead we have a slate, and when she says so, we can write and even draw on it. We can wipe off what we have done with a piece of dirty wet rag. I am glad of that. I don't like to see what I have written.

She shows us the letters and we write them down. We learn that C.A.T. spells cat, and all sorts of other little words, and Miss Lord writes a lot of them on the blackboard and we can read them. And we do numbers up to twenty and it is all easy.

When I grow up, I think I would like to be a teacher and have a blackboard.

After lunch Miss Lord tells us a story, and we put our heads down on the desk and have a rest and all is peaceful and quiet.

After I steal the lily and am labelled thief, I lie low, but I keep doing all the good things they show you how to do. I don't feel like a thief over the lily, because the lady had so many of them, I'm sure she wouldn't even have noticed that one was gone, and anyway they were just growing there in the ground, for anyone to take.

Sometimes I even get praised for my work. I am now more wary of Miss Lord, and I never take flowers again, and I am beginning to understand that at school, as well as at home, you have to watch your step and do as you're told. But I begin to feel that I am loving school, and that it makes up for the piano, and I worry in case they find out that I am enjoying it and am good at it, and say I shouldn't have it and take it away from me. Then I remember about the truancy officer, and with a small secret thrill of triumph I know that they won't be able to stop me.

Jock has been left down in his grade because he can't do the work, so when I am put up into grade one I am in his grade. I sit next to him and show him how to do it. Much later he will claim that he was the one who showed me, but this is my story, and I am telling it as I remember it, and I know I was the one who helped him.

Halfway through the year, a man comes into our room. He is the head. He extracts the five boys who have been kept down in grade one for a second year. He says they are too old for the grade and moves them up to grade two.

By lunchtime I have been deposed.

'Ya! Ya! Who got left down?' shouts Jock from the other side of the road, where he is walking with a bigger boy. 'You're stupid! You got left down!'

I am enraged. It isn't fair! I taught him how to do it and now he is put up and I am left down! Now I'm the stupid one!

I go home howling to Mother, who gives me short shrift. She is delighted that Jock has been put up ('It was a mistake to leave him down in the first place, such a bright boy,' she tells neighbours and friends) and tells me to stop my nonsense. Eventually she softens a bit.

'Education is for boys, not for girls, and you can't both have it,' she says. 'Girls only grow up and get married, and it is all wasted.'

But I think of the truant officer. Nothing will stop me this time.

ONE NIGHT

THE MEMORIES don't flow along smoothly like a train on its rails. They dart about like dragonflies on water, or like swallows in the eaves, and there seems no hope of pinning them down. But if I write, something from yesterday triggers another, apparently unrelated memory today, and they go back and back until a lot of the little pieces begin to fit together, and I have enough little pieces to make some sort of a picture.

Way, way back, there has been a telegram, saying: MISSING, BELIEVED KILLED.

And one night, when I am lying in bed with Mother, well-fed warm and contented, there are loud frightening noises — a man is banging at the back door and roaring: 'Open the door, or I'll break it down!'

'He's come back from the dead!' shrieks Mother.

Then he is in the room.

'She's taken my place!' he roars and he throws me out of bed.

There are people there, and police, and the man is gone.

I have my first visit to hospital, and from deep down I hear a sawing noise as two men open up the back of my head.

'Depressed fracture of the skull. She'll never be any good after this!' says one of them. 'I don't know why we bother.'

At home the man comes and he goes.

'He came back from the war a changed man,' says Mother. And she blames me.

'This is all your fault!' she cries at me. 'If you hadn't been born, none of this would have happened!'

The times before the man comes are the best times of all. When he is not there, it is Uncle George who comes every afternoon. He is the first one, the one who is there soon after the very beginning, when the doctor says: 'It's a girl!' and hands me over to the matron. The matron offers me to Mother. 'Do you want her?' she asks.

'No, I don't. But her father will want to see her when he comes in this afternoon.'

It is red-haired Uncle George, Daddy's much older brother, who comes in the afternoon. He is delighted. He has been married to Auntie Sis for fifteen years and everybody knows he can't have any children.

'Is she really mine?' he asks.

'There's been no-one else,' says Mother, wryly.

'She's beautiful!' he says, and it always seems to me that Uncle George is the one who belongs with us, not the man.

But Mother says to herself: 'I'll have to get rid of her before Rex comes home, or he'll kill the pair of us!'

Uncle George keeps coming every afternoon, and it is a very happy time for all of us. He brings us chocolates and ginger beer in a stone bottle, and special presents for me. He calls me his baby. He gives me a gold chain bracelet, with my name EMMA on a little gold heart dangling from it, so I know who I am. He buys me a new dress, and a sleeping-doll with a china face and real hair. I want to call the doll Mary, but Jennie says its name is Desiree, which I think is a silly name.

'Do what Jennie tells you!' Mother always says, 'she's the eldest!'

So Desiree it is.

'It should have been mine!' says Jennie angrily. 'I'm the eldest!'

'Uncle George loves me. He gave it to me because I am his baby!' I say.

After that Jennie is very angry. Mother is even more angry.

'He doesn't come to see you, he comes to see me!' she says.

Now she starts shutting me out in the yard when Uncle George comes.

'She's got too much to say for herself,' she says.

'Couldn't you just put her down for a sleep?' asks Uncle.

'She's too old to have a sleep in the daytime!' says Mother.

Mother gets a letter from a lady in Southampton in England. She got Mother's address from Daddy's wallet when he was asleep. She wrote that she was having Daddy's child and she wanted Mother's help to get him to support her.

'Get rid of her,' screams Mother.

Daddy seems frightened and goes berserk.

'Where is the letter?' he roars. 'Where have you put it?' and he starts tearing the place apart till he finds, hidden under the big black marble clock on the mantelpiece, not that piece of paper but another one. This paper is about me being born; the date tells him that I am not his child. He was in Malta when I was started.

Then it is Mother's turn to be frightened. 'She was late!' says Mother, but he doesn't believe her.

'I'm not having another man's bastard in my house,' he yells, 'taking the bread out of my mouth! I can't look after the ones I've got, let alone somebody else's! Get rid of her! That's woman's work! Get rid of her!'

Mother comes into the room where I now sleep one night and puts her hand over my face so that I can't breathe. I struggle and squirm, but it is a half-hearted attempt on her part, and she goes back to Daddy in the bedroom and says: 'You'll have to do it. I can't.'

She tells Uncle George that I am Daddy's baby, not his, and after that it is Uncle George who goes away and Daddy who stays.

'She should never have been allowed to see the light of day!' he mutters as he leaves.

Mother can't bear to look at me after what she has done.

Now it is Daddy who gets up to me in the night if I cry.

'Stop that crying, now!' he says, when he gets up to me. 'I'm your mother now, and if you don't do as I say, you won't eat. You're living on my charity!'

And now it is I myself who start doing the bad things.

The first bad thing I do is that I talk to Daddy about Mother taking my breath away. I only begin dimly to understand that telling about it was a bad thing when Daddy laughs and says: 'Now I've got her!'

And I think: 'I will never say anything bad about my mother again!'

The next bad thing I do is that I talk to Mother about Daddy.

I talk about things I have seen.

I tell about Daddy.

He is in a little room, I say, with a lot of beds in it, some of them one on top of the other.

A lot of men are shouting at Daddy because of his kitbag.

'What's in it?' they say. 'It stinks! Get rid of it!'

Daddy won't. He even has it in bed with him.

They say they are going to tell the captain.

As soon as they are gone, Daddy is in a hurry. He takes out what is in the bag. It is a lady's head, all black and with hair sticking out all round it. He pushes it out the little round window in the wall, and forces the kitbag through the window after it.

The captain comes back with the men.

'What's in the bag?' he asks. 'Where is it?'

Daddy is very angry. 'It was expensive underclothes for my wife,' he says. 'I bought them in Cairo. Spent all my pay on them. Now some bastard's pinched them! And my kitbag too.'

All this out loud I tell, one sunny morning in the kitchen, with my eyes half shut and everybody staring at me and nobody moving.

Suddenly Daddy starts to scream.

'She's a witch! She's talking about things that happened before she was even born! Things she couldn't possibly know about! She's crazy!' And to me: 'How do you know such things? Who have you been talking to? Tell me! Tell me! Or I'll shake the living daylights out of you!' And he shakes me and shakes me till I come back from where I have been, and I am very frightened.

'I don't know how I know,' I stammer at last, from the floor where I have fallen. 'It just came out of your head into my head. I think you told me, but you said not to tell anyone, only I forgot.'

And Mother takes Daddy's arm. 'Calm down, Rex! Calm down! It's just her imagination! Nobody would believe that!'

Daddy calms down, and he says to me: 'Nobody's going to believe such yarns! If you ever tell anyone such things, they'll lock you up and throw away the key.'

And when we are alone, he says, close to my face: 'If ever I see you talking to your mother again, I'll kill you. I'll see to it that you never forget again.'

I never tell anyone what I have seen again. I keep seeing other things — I can't help it — but I keep them all to myself.

I have seen a lady in England, where Daddy's ship goes. She is in a place with white stuff all over the ground, and black trees with no leaves. She has done what Daddy told her to do; she has brought all the money she can get hold of so they can go away together. But Daddy takes his big army knife thing and cuts the lady's head off, and there is red blood all over the white stuff.

'I'll take it home, so she'll know what will happen to her if she even looks at another man,' he says, and he puts her head in his kitbag and goes back and hides on the ship till it sails.

The first time I start seeing things, it is a lady in France, no, the lady in France is the second one.

The first one is when Daddy is still a big boy, wearing apple-catchers tucked into his long socks. He is walking with a big girl on a path beside the sea. She is saying: 'I'll have to tell my mother,' and he pushes her over the cliffs onto the rocks below. The police ask him a lot of questions, and he says she tripped and fell, and they don't quite believe him but they don't do anything.

I have seen a lady in France, in the war. He sticks her with his big army knife thing as they lie in bed together, and she screams and screams. Other soldiers start running out of the house, then there is a terrible loud noise and the house is burning.

Daddy told me that story before I stopped talking to him, after the last time I ever asked him a question.

'Daddy,' I asked him, 'why have you only got one of those ball things down there, when Jock and the baby have got two?'

'You've seen too much!' he says. 'You'll have to go!'

But he tells me that after they bombed the house and set fire to it, so no-one would know it was the Australians who did it, the other men crowded round him and got him down and cut one of them off — 'to teach him a lesson' — so he wouldn't ever do it again.

'She wasn't even dead,' he tells me, 'and as we drove away in the truck, I could hear her screaming and screaming. And sometimes in my head I can still hear her screaming in the burning house and I can never get away from it.'

And I feel very sorry for him.

'Why did you do it to her?' I ask. 'What had she done?'

He is very angry. 'She was a tart!' he says.

'Daddy,' I say, 'her life was just as important to her as yours is to you!'

'She was a tart!' he says again, 'just a tart!' and he says it in a way that makes me feel I must be stupid because I can't see it.

So I ask him again: 'Daddy: why do you do it? All those ladies?'

'It gives me a thrill,' he says. 'It's better than sex. It's better than anything!'

I do not understand.

It wasn't only ladies that I saw. There were men too.

The first picture with men in it is in a sort of dark passage — with walls made of dirt, with water dripping down the sides. Daddy and another soldier are arguing. Daddy owes him some money from poker. He is going to tell the captain. Daddy takes something and points it at his face and suddenly, bang! he has no face. Other men come running.

'He just took his gun and shot himself!' says Daddy. 'Must've all got too much for him!'

I have seen another man standing on some boards with the sea all around. Again there is an argument about money. Daddy turns round, then comes back and makes a rush at him and he is over the side and into the sea.

*　　*　　*

The last story is not about killing. It is about me. It is the worst story, for me, because I am in it, and Mother and Daddy are both in it too.

I am just big enough to be in a proper bed all for myself. In the middle of the night, when I am asleep, the shouting and screaming starts again. The screaming is Mother, about Daddy's drinking and gambling and all the money gone.

'We're going to lose the house because of your gambling!' she screams.

The shouting is Daddy saying: 'You're out of your mind! They'll take your children away from you if you carry on like that! They'll lock you up and throw away the key!'

The door slams and Daddy comes into my room, so I ask him for threepence to buy Mother a new house and he gives it to me. Then he gets into bed with me and touches me. I don't want him to touch me, because I think that touching me down there might give me a baby, and I am not big enough for a baby yet. But he pushes my hands away and touches me anyway.

In the morning I give Mother the threepence to buy the new house.

'Where did you get it?'

'Daddy gave it to me. And he touched me down there, and it gave me a lovely feeling.'

And suddenly there is more screaming, and this time it is at me.

'The money's not his! It's mine!' she screams at me. 'And you dare to tell me you let him touch you! And that you enjoyed it! You're a bad, bad girl! You're a filthy little slut! I'll kill him! I'll kill the pair of you!' And she is hitting me round the head and I am crying too.

'She's a little liar!' says Daddy. 'I never touched her! And I never gave her any money! She must have pinched it out of my pocket!'

Later Mother says to me: 'I don't know how you can ever enjoy yourself again, after what you've done!'

It is not clear to me what it is I have done that is so bad.

Is it seeing things?

Is it asking for the money?

Is it talking to Mother?

Is it talking to Daddy?

Is it letting Daddy touch me?

Is it saying it was a lovely feeling?

I get another message from Mother — or is it from inside myself? I am no longer quite sure — a message that says to me deep down: 'Don't ever let him touch you again! Don't look at him! Don't even talk to him! Or he'll do to you what he did to all those other women.'

But wherever the message comes from, I feel I am in a very dangerous place, and nobody wants me.

OUT OF THE SHADOWS

IT IS Christmas.

I have come home from hospital where I could not stay because there was no staff. I am very sick, needing constant attention, and incontinent. Mother gives me morphia pills in the daytime, but at night Daddy takes over and refuses to give me the pills because they will make me a drug addict. I am awake screaming all night, with no morphia to deaden the pain. It is a nightmare time for us all.

Mother is distraught.

'I can't look after her! She's too heavy to lift!'

The doctor's prophecies for my future promise only what Daddy puts into words for Mother: 'She's nothing but a vegetable! She's not even human. She's going to be a millstone round your neck for the rest of your life. You'll be better off without her.'

And as I stubbornly refuse to die, they collude to rid themselves of this appalling liability.

'Once she gets to school, they'll have a record of

her and if she doesn't show up, there'll be someone asking questions. So we'd better get on with it.'

They make two more attempts on my life before they give up.

First Daddy crushes a box of Beecham's pills into a glass of milk and makes me drink it. I spew it up, and soon the doctor is there.

(Did Mother send for him yet again?)

The doctor coaxes me to drink something else horrible, which makes me spew all the more, but he is pleased, pats me on the head, calls me 'Good girl' and encourages me to drink some more and spew some more.

'Let it all out!' he says.

'Don't know how she could have got hold of those!' says my good Daddy. 'The kids must have given them to her.'

The next attempt is the last.

In a long pram, lent to them by the hospital, they push me very late one night to a spot beside the St Kilda pier, and Daddy tries to drown me in the icy cold sea.

'As soon as the tide turns it will wash her out to sea, and the sharks will have her before morning,' he says. 'And if there's no body, you can't be charged.'

But I cling to him in terror and with such tenacity that he begins to lose his footing and I nearly topple him into the water.

'She's going to pull me under with her!' he cries in a frenzy, as he desperately tries to free himself from my clutching hands. *'She's trying to drown me!'*

A man is passing by — surely a miracle, at that hour, on that cold deserted beach — who hears the noise and comes running over to see what the commotion's about.

Daddy explains it very simply: 'My wife and I went for a little walk together, and her pram rolled . . .'

It is too dangerous to try again.

'She'll probably die of pneumonia before the week's out!' he says.

I don't get pneumonia and I don't die.

'You couldn't kill that kid with a bloody axe!' he says in disgust, and he gives up.

He concentrates now on making sure that I don't tell what happened, and indeed for a long time he is quite safe, because I have no conscious memory of that lost weekend at all.

'When the dust settles,' he says, 'she'll do just what she's told, like everybody else.'

I go back to hospital and it is months before I come home the second time. The slash marks on my face have been repaired, and my face looks like a face again. My hair has grown short and spiky, and I can walk again, though my movements are very stiff and jerky (*I can't bear to look at her! She's like a bloody wind-up toy!*) and I have to lie on the floor every day and do the exercises they taught me in hospital to make me more supple.

The contraption that wired up my broken jaw has gone, but I still can't talk. I have in my head a not-yet conscious prophecy from the good doctor that tells me: 'She'll never talk again, from what I hear.' And I am convinced that this is so.

It will be Mrs McPhee from primary school who, much later, frees me from this conviction, when she teaches us to sing. I become aware one day at school that I am singing with the other kids, and that what I am singing is *words*, and that I can have the words just like everybody else. And though the first words I say sound like a rusty gate creaking, and I use them only at school and never at home, and though everyone is startled when I begin to speak at first, I am talking at last.

And nobody tells on me!

When I come home from hospital the second time, all this is still a long way off. It is a comfort to me that I have a life-line, in the shape of a series of out-patient appointments at the hospital, to the good doctor who would not let me die (though I am forbidden to talk to him) and who had mended my sores, my stab wounds, my bites, and my broken and dislocated bones. And it is a comfort, too, that I do not have to sleep alone, but share a sleep-out with Jock and Jennie.

Daddy has explained my injuries to the relations: 'She tripped and fell down the stairs. She wasn't like that when they took her away! Those doctors at the hospital have done that to her! Lot of bloody butchers!'

He has issued a set of instructions to Mother and Jennie and Jock:

'Nobody's to help her. She's got to learn to do things for herself.'

'Nobody's to talk to her, or you'll get what she got.'

'And don't listen to her, or she'll have you as mad as she is.'

I don't want anyone to get what I got, so I don't even try to talk to them, but when nobody talks and nobody listens to me, I feel that I am not really there at all.

Later Daddy relents. 'We'll have to let someone talk to her, or she'll go crazy and be even more trouble. Let Jock talk to her. He can keep her in order!'

So Jock becomes the only one I can talk to — my only ally.

Once or twice Daddy is forced to realise that even if I don't talk, at some level I have some memory of what happened.

One cold Sunday morning, the first clear memory of something that had happened that night opens up. While Mother and Daddy are still asleep, and we three are out of bed but creeping around and playing very quietly so as not to wake them, I suddenly notice the two deep drawers at the bottom of the wardrobe.

'Those two big drawers are the ones he was going to put me in after —'

Before I can even finish my thought, Daddy is in our room, in a dark and silent rage, taking my temperature, which is down, and roaring: 'What are you doing out of bed? Get back to bed and stay there!'

Rightly or wrongly, I am convinced that he has read my mind, and it is not even safe to think any more.

Daddy once made some sort of apology to me for what had happened, but at the time I had little conscious memory of it all and I didn't know what he was talking about. His words had no more significance for me than pebbles dropping into the deep unfathomable pool of my mind.

'It was the whisky, Em. The whisky and the pills.'

The pills were cocaine, obtained while he was, as Jennie said, 'a sort of doctor' — a medical orderly in the army medical service.

Another time: 'Your mother made me.'

And: 'It was another man who did that to you, Em.'

And finally: 'I thought you were someone else.'

(The time will come when I will remember that last excuse and give one of my mighty hoots of unsuitable laughter, and even be comforted and gasp: 'Well, it's nice to know it was nothing personal!')

Inside me somewhere there is the me who *knew* that Daddy did not do it. My Daddy would not do such things. Nobody would believe things. Mother said so, when I first told the stories about the ship. And besides, if he had, he wouldn't have said he didn't, or God would have struck him dead for telling lies.

Inside me is the me who wasn't sure I had arrived home to the right family.

Inside me is the me who is perhaps dead (everyone says so), and for whom dead might be better, because when you're dead you feel no pain.

But inside me too is the me in the morgue, who was afraid of being buried alive and who said: '*I am not dead! Get me down! I won't die!*'

Inside me there is still the me who knows who I am — I am Emma, as my name on the little gold heart on the bracelet Uncle George gave me said.

No-one else.

And though I want so much to believe that my Daddy would not do such things, when I do remember, I remember that Friday morning on my fourth birthday and the night which followed it.

I remember walking to the station, and Mother holding up her face to be kissed as she gets on the train with Jennie and Jock. They are going to the Scottish Grandma's, where I can't yet go. (*I won't have her in my house if she's not your husband's child!*)

'Go straight home,' says Mother, 'and don't talk to anyone. Go into the house and stay inside, so nobody knows you're there. I'll be home in the morning and I'll bring you a birthday present. Your father will be home at tea-time. He'll look after you.'

When the train goes and I am left alone, I don't go straight home; I play on the railway bridge — up a few steps, down a few steps, up to the top to look down on the next train, then hopping down on one leg, so that I nearly fall. A man is watching me.

'Where's your mother?' he asks.

'She's out!' I say, as cheekily as I dare.

'You should go home to your mother,' he says.

Another one who doesn't believe me! But I go home. The blinds are all down. There is nothing to do. I wander about. I look at the picture books for a long while. I get hungry. I go to the kitchen and hack a piece of bread off the loaf and spread it with butter and honey. The table — Mother's beautiful white scrubbed wooden table — is soon a mess. I think of the man at the station who I shouldn't have talked to, and I know I am in trouble. I am a bad, bad girl! But I lie on Mother's bed, on her beautiful flowery quilt — another big no-no — and look at the picture books again for a long time. I go to sleep. And that night after it got dark on my fourth birthday I remember waking up to hear the big key turning the lock in the back door, and how I laughed when he put the light on and I saw the man, because he looked so funny. He was staggering all over the place, and his thing, all swollen and sore-looking, was hanging out of the unbuttoned front of his trousers. And when I looked at his face I stopped laughing, because his face *was* Daddy's face yet it was *not* Daddy's face. It was wild and dark and different.

And the man had only one testicle.

EPILOGUE

ONLY CONNECT!

THE TASK of recovering my internalised memories, of separating what *they* said from what really happened, of listening to my own voice and becoming myself again, has been a long and difficult and painful one.

The nurses and doctors at the hospital who saved my life, who mended my broken body so that it has served me well for so long, and who did a lot to keep alive my faith in the essential goodness of the human race, were themselves human beings too, and limited by their society and the limitations it put on them.

The concept that my damaged soul, or psyche, was as much in need of healing as my body did not yet exist, so nobody even tried. It is now recognised that the longer the time that elapses between the actual trauma and the psychotherapy needed to treat the trauma, the longer and more difficult the process will be.

So I forgive myself for taking so long!

The analyst had said to me: 'If you can't talk, perhaps you could write it down?'

Before I could even write it down, I had to deal with the memory of that first writing lesson, when I had been made to write that I had stabbed the baby because I was jealous, and with my own confusion about what had happened then.

When I listened to myself, I knew that I had not stabbed the baby; I had loved the baby and tried to save him when they were stabbing him with the scissors. But I had to deal also with my own guilt at having told a lie, at saying that I had killed the baby when I hadn't, and fear too, in case God would strike me dead — had nearly struck me dead?

I had not killed anyone. I was not dangerous, except insofar as I had realised when I saw my daughter sitting on Daddy's knee and doing what I had done, as she lovingly stroked the 'hole in his face' — the dimple in his chin — that I would kill anyone who did to her, or any of my children, what Daddy had done to me. And I will remember with a nervous giggle, an old memory dating from after I stopped going to the out-patient department at the hospital as a child, of my feeling that I *would like to do something myself, instead of being always the one things were done to. But what could I do? Kill the lot of them? But then nobody would be happy! And in my head I scream at them: 'Why can't you help each other instead of always screaming and shouting and killing?'*

So I wrote the first two chapters about a mythical little girl — Not-Me! The little girl of the first two chapters was the Not-Me I had disowned when I first looked down from somewhere above at my dirty disgusting twisted stabbed and broken body on the floor. She was the scarred me that I saw in the mirror that Jennie brought me when I first came home from hospital, and I disowned me again. 'That's not me!'

It was the task of owning those me-s and connecting them with the now-me that has taken so long and been so difficult and painful.

E.M. Forster, of *Passage to India* fame, showed me how.

'Only connect!' he said. So those bloody books that made me such a useless head-in-the-clouds creature in my teens served some purpose after all!

Though I had for a long time kept a diary, I didn't begin writing this book seriously until after I retired. I started a writing course at Holmsglen College of Tafe, still carrying a great load of underground baggage: *I'll never live to tell the tale if I write anything about Daddy. I shouldn't be here. Anything I write will be a load of garbage. Nobody will want to publish it. Nobody will believe a word of it! If you tell anyone that stuff, they'll lock you up and throw away the key! Dragging out all that stuff is morbid in the extreme. Get on with your life and forget all about it.*

And I will remember the policeman: 'Who did this to you?'

'I don't remember I don't remember I don't remember —'

And as soon as I remember, he'll do it again! So I'm never going to remember!

But when I do remember, I will remember that I was at Auntie's the night after the doctor had been and that Daddy smothered the baby with the pillow.

And from Mother: 'He's my husband and the father of my children, and I mustn't say a word against him.'

For too long I simply could not bear to look at that time, to go back to it, to even think of it.

'Why don't you listen to *yourself*?' the analyst had asked.

Because inside me was still a too-trusting me who believed what *they* said and blotted out the parts that I could not bear to remember.

Because inside me was still the me who had said to Daddy the night before he almost killed me: 'I heard you and Mother talking last night and saying you were going to kill me. I'm frightened.'

But I still *wanted* to believe the Daddy who had replied: 'We wouldn't harm you. We love you. We'll look after you!'

That me believed the Daddy who said: 'She was asking for it. She brought it on herself, the way she went on, the way she sat on my knee stroking the dimple in my chin and saying, "Oh, you poor man, you've got a hole in your face."'

So when the analyst, in answer to my statement that I had been in hospital as a very small child, had asked: 'What happened to you?,' I answered quickly with the family myth: 'Nothing happened!'

And I can now finish that sentence with the rest of the family myth: 'Nothing happened! It was all lies! I made it all up! It was just my imagination!'

And it was easier to believe that than to believe that they had not wanted me, that they'd be better off without me, that I was the cause of all the trouble. That in spite of what Mother had said, there really are people who do such terrible things, and my stepfather was one of them, not just Goths, Vandals and Huns, not just Nazis, but men here in our own society, men who knew that asbestos killed, that tobacco killed, and kept that knowledge secret to make money.

But the analyst asked me my maiden name and went away and researched the hospital records. And he saw the me-on-the-floor. The me I could not bear to look at myself, or let anyone else see. The me so badly damaged that, as Daddy had said, nobody who saw it would ever be able to love me again. And I saw that he saw.

The analyst said to me: *'Why don't you listen to yourself?'*

And I almost hated him.

I hated him for Daddy, who was, according to Jennie, a sort of doctor. I hated him for the succession of doctors who had said: 'She'll never be any good after this!' I even hated him for the good doctor, the doctor of the morgue, who had acted on the Hippocratic oath and had certainly saved my life. But who seemed to betray me when he sent me back to them, twice. He sent me back so they could try again! Having no alternative, the now-me realises.

But the now-me remembers that I said to myself that I wasn't going to believe all those doctors who said I'd never be any good after this.

And though I knew I was being unreasonable, that one of my wants had been to know what happened, I hated and feared the analyst doctor at the beginning because he was making me remember, and a deep self-protective part of me knew it was still too dangerous to remember. The underground me, who would not yet remember the early stuff, half remembered and feared the Daddy who I could not entirely repress, who had killed Harry when he threatened to tell Mother that Daddy said: 'You can't have Jennie! I've been fucking her for years!' That Daddy was still alive and saying to me with his forked tongue: 'You'd better be careful, Emma. You've got children now!'

Why couldn't the analyst just agree with me, give me back the shield behind which I'd hidden all those years? If he'd just agree with me, say to me what I'd accepted — that it was all my fault, but it was all in the past, and as long as I never did anything like that again, then everything would be all right.

But the analyst had seen the me-on-the-floor. The me I could not bear to look at myself. And he knew it was true.

The analyst said to me again: *'Why don't you listen to yourself?'*

And I almost hated him.

Why couldn't he do what the skin specialist had done when he bullied me into realising that the

Relaxatab I had taken was a drug? Why couldn't he bully me into telling about whatever crimes I had committed — had I stabbed a baby? killed someone? been a three-year-old slut? — just so whatever I had done would be out in the open and I would be free of it.

Perhaps he realised I'd been bullied too often.

Why didn't I listen to myself?

Because whatever I'd said, I was told that it was all lies, just my imagination or, as my only ally, Jock, said: 'What would you know about it? You're only a girl!'

Listening to myself was not a skill I had learned. It was more important to listen to them. My life had depended on it for too many years.

But inside me, that small voice that had stirred and spoken when I came to after the bang on the head from the garage doors, was stirring again. My own voice — the me that after Jennie's breakdown had sent me to the analyst because I knew I must have help — my own voice told me that *I could trust this man, and that he would help me, if I let him.*

But — but — (Nobody's to help her! Anybody who helps her will get what she got!) And I did not want anyone to get what I got! I could not risk it!

And listening to myself involved reconciling not only the then-Mother with the later Mothers, the then-Daddy with the later Daddies, the then-Jock with the later Jocks, the then-Jennie with the later ones, but also the then-me with the now-me.

The lovely Mother I had lain beside as a baby and felt safe and secure with was also the Mother who had tried to abort me and had said to the matron: 'I don't want her' on the day I was born.

She was the terrifying Mother who'd said: 'I'll kill the pair of you!' when I told her Daddy had touched me. Who combined with Daddy to get rid of me when I became a threat to them both. Me with my big mouth! Me with my total recall! Me with my photographic memory!

Mother was also the beautiful Mother in the floral nightie and the long brown dress who'd come in the night and taken my breath away, so that fear was always there too.

She was the Mother who had colluded half-heartedly with Daddy (because *Nobody says 'No' to me and lives?*) in those attempts to kill me with the pills and in the sea at St Kilda.

She was the Mother who sent for the doctors to save me.

She was the Mother who said, finally, to Daddy: *'If you touch any of those children again, I'll kill you!'*

She was the Mother who fed me delicious food, who nursed me, however angrily and unwillingly, back to health after I came home from hospital the second time.

She was the Mother who was part of the rush at me that put me in hospital after I opened the garage doors. She was also the Mother who'd said 'I want her back!' and could at last bear to look at me again when I came home from that hospital. She was the one who had bought me the vieux rose dress and had admired me in it.

On the night Harry died, when I got up out of bed after I heard the truck leave and offered to help her clean up the blood, she was the Mother who said to me: 'Go back to bed and don't let him know you know.' And I could not *not know* any longer. 'It's him! It's the same man! It's not "another man"! We'll never be safe again!'

But Harry's death had done something for me.

When I went back to school that lunchtime, I let go.

I cried.

Out loud.

In front of the whole class at the central school, I cried. I let go.

I said not a word, but I cried.

I cried a cry from my deepest depths.

I cried for the first time since the death of my baby brother, Onda Dord, the child born of the rape on Mother by the man up the street who had come to fix the blocked sink.

And I was somehow released and able to move on.

I said to Mother: 'I don't like him any more!'

She said: 'He's your father, Em.'

As though it was not permissible *not* to love your 'father', no matter what he did.

And I think I saw then that Mother would always do what Daddy told her. And I cut myself off from her, too.

I've done a lot of crying since then.

Eventually I have cried for her, and her fear of Daddy, her fear of what people would say, for her illnesses and her awful life, for there being no-one she could turn to, not even her own mother, for her being married to Daddy, as well as for the awful things she herself said and did and allowed to be done. And for the me to whom those things were said and done.

I respect her right to try and abort me when she had committed the at that time unforgivable sin of adultery resulting in a birth.

But I knew then that I, too, had a right to live, and that somehow I would find a way to live.

And with that terrible sense of humour of mine, I can't help a wry laugh at her bad luck — that when her husband was pronounced missing, believed killed, she sought solace from the one man who was known to be unable to beget children — her brother-in-law — and bingo! Me!

I realise that she damaged me seriously when she kept insisting that I was Daddy's child and prevented me from being loved by Uncle George or anybody else, in case I told the truth about my conception, or that she had tried to smother me, or the truth about Daddy and what he did to me.

Nobody should have to keep secrets like that.

Now my revelations will not harm anybody.

When I was driving past the Coburg cemetery one day with my youngest daughter, I said to her: 'That's where my mother is buried.'

My then ten-year-old daughter was shocked.

'Why don't you ever go and put flowers on her grave?' she asked.

'Because the part of my mother that I loved is not there,' I said.

At last I cry for Jennie, who, as she had been taught, thought it all right to try to kill me, the little sister whom 'everybody loved', when I supplanted her. Who did not understand that Uncle George had his own reasons for preferring me. Who blamed only herself when Daddy had intercourse with her on the bathroom floor.

And eventually I cry for that little three-year-old me, who didn't know what to believe or who to trust. Who had believed Mother when she said: 'It's all your fault! If you hadn't been born, none of this would have happened.'

And though the last part of that sentence is partly true, the first part is not.

And when I realise that, I can bear to accept the me-on-the-floor and stop minding that people can see me, because it was *not all my fault*.

As I understand how easy it was for a sophisticated experienced unscrupulous charmer to exploit his fifteen-year-old daughter, I see how much easier it was for him to seduce a three-year-old child. At last I realise that the responsibility in both cases was with him.

What I felt for him was so complex!

I had been sorry for him when he'd screamed because he couldn't look after another man's bastard when he couldn't even look after the children he had. I thought I loved him, but when I remember the things he did to me, I do not understand how I could have. I only know that it was vital that I did not arouse his displeasure — their displeasure. That surely is fear, rather than love. Yet as long as I managed to push aside all the bad stuff, I had been able to love him for his charm, for the fish and chips, for the talk, even though his early talk had filled my brain with horror stories, in which he had the murderer's part. Were they just horror stories, like those in the Grimm's fairy tales? Until Harry died I could believe it, as I had wanted to. But not after I had seen Harry's blood.

After that I could only pretend to believe it, and try to blot it out.

As long as I could blot out the rest, I could love him for the nights he got up and put poultices on my abscesses when I was in fifth form. For the times he praised me. For the way he had of making a woman — any woman — feel she was important. For the fact that he went to work and his efforts fed me and clothed me and put a roof over my head and allowed me to stay at school till I qualified. For the nice old man he seemed to be when he was old, till he died in bed, not without ructions, at Jennie's place.

Until I let my mind remember too, my body remembered. My body was afraid of stairs. Of pen-knives. Of falling. Of loud noises. My body had pains in the side, where he had dislocated my hip as he dragged me down the stairs. The back of my head gave me sharp pains when I heard a sawing noise. My chest constricted, as though I was under a heavy weight or in mortal terror, when I heard Daddy's — any man's — loud angry shouting. Until they started using injections, I fought anaesthetists off (as I had tried to fight Daddy off) when they put pads soaked with ether on my face and said: 'Repeat after me . . .' and a series of numbers, as they did in those days.

I will even have the courage to remember and accept as mine the words that accompanied that powerful murderous feeling I had when I saw him with my little daughter on his knee, stroking the hole in his face: *'If anyone did to any of my daughters what he did to me, I'd kill him!'*

And it was the power and violence of that thought — as yet unrelated to the remembrance that produced it — that made me realise I needed help.

When I was growing up, there was a wonderful recording of a 'fruity melodrama' played over and over again on the radio.

It told of one Topsy, I think, tied to the railway lines by a moustachioed villain. (After Daddy shaved his off, he had warned me against ever trusting a man with a moustache, because, he said, he's got something to hide. Poor Ronald Colman! Poor Clark Gable! I never could quite trust them!) I forget all the details of Topsy's rescue, but the record finished with the line:

'We will look forward to the bright and glorious future that lies ahead.'

My tidy, basically logical mind saw that as a good aim. I wanted all those untidy, unclean, dangerous bits packed away, tied neatly, preferably with a bow. I wanted my bills paid, my children clean, healthy, safe, well-educated and happy. I wanted my past tucked away in a drawer, labelled past, and preferably locked.

A little on the unrealistic side, I must agree. My memory, after all, is part of me, and how I deal with it makes me what I am. My resistance to pills, which I saw as dangerous (they'd tried to kill me with them, and Daddy had told of doctors in the army who'd given people pills to shut them up if they screamed!), was also a resistance to the understanding that pills would dull my memory so that I would never be able to remember, and so would never be able to be free of my fears.

And my children, thank God!, all turned out to have minds of their own, and almost as much skill at passive resistance, and much better skills at open resistance when it was called for, than I'd had myself.

And all my wants!

I wanted a garden when I grew up, with freesias in it, like the dentist's next door to one of the innumerable houses of my childhood.

I wanted to feel safe to love and be loved.

I wanted everyone to be happy.

I wanted an education.

I wanted a career.

I wanted to do what the others did, as long as I didn't have to kill anyone!

I wanted to get married and have children, in that order.

I wanted to somehow subvert the Old Testament edict: 'The sins of the fathers will be visited on the children,' as I had seen done in my own childhood.

I wanted to write a book — to tell my story.

I wanted to know what had happened, way back then.

I wanted *not* to know what happened, way back then.

We have to be very careful about what we want — and what we don't want!

Writing this book was the last 'want' I tackled. Perhaps the hardest, because it involved listening to myself and jettisoning a lot of what had seemed self-evident truths until I could stop accepting what they said, that it was all lies! all my imagination!

I have told, and I am still alive. It has been a long journey, and often a painful one. I am past blaming them, because I do not know how I would have behaved in their shoes.

I have had in many ways a very good life. I have wonderful daughters and grand-daughters. I have had a successful career teaching in both state and independent secondary schools. I have friends.

Some people won't believe my story.

There is still a powerful group of health professionals who deny the truth of recovered memory and classify it all as childhood fantasies. They point out, rightly, that such memories are often recovered only after those who could verify or disprove them have died.

And I answer: 'Well, of course! Wouldn't you wait till then?'

I have told my story, as best I can.

And now that I have told it, I can laugh and cry again, be angry, be sad, be happy, love and be loved, be stupid, be intelligent, be weak, be strong, be scared, be brave, be right, be wrong. Be human.

I am not Caesar's wife, I do not have to be perfect.

I still have a diabolical sense of humour, sometimes!

I am alive.

I am glad to be alive.